CW01670036

Best wishes
Norman
Bobby Kerr

ACKNOWLEDGEMENTS

First of all, I am indebted to Brian Leng who has worked alongside me throughout the writing of this book and particularly for helping me recall so many of the memories which have, shall we say, become a little vague with the passing of time. I'm certain he knows infinitely more about my football career than I ever will!

My special thanks also go to Paul and Louise Briggs of twocan. Their graphic design skills have ensured that the story of my life in football and beyond has been presented in a truly grand fashion.

I am also indebted to my good friend Jim Montgomery for writing the foreword for the book and also my former Sunderland colleagues and personal friends too numerous to mention for their input and support throughout the project.

SPECIAL THANKS

My special thanks must go to The Tim Rice Charitable Trust, Hays Travel, John Craggs and the staff at Gentoo, Olivers Dental Studio, Harry Green, Aiden Moran, Tallulah Moran Ganley, Marcus and Guy Harris and the Davis family at the Copt Hill.

a twocan publication

©2013. Published by twocan.

Every effort has been made to ensure the accuracy of information within this publication but the publishers can not be held responsible for any errors or omissions. Views expressed are those of the author and do not necessarily represent those of the publishers. All rights reserved.

ISBN 978-0-9569879-3-8

PICTURES: Action Images, Blackpool Pictures, Getty Images, Mirrorpix, North East Press, Press Association & SAFC.

the little general

Bobby Kerr's football scrapbook

Bobby Kerr with Brian Leng

S

First of all let me say how delighted I was when I was asked to write the foreword for this book. I've known Bobby since he first arrived at Roker Park back in the summer of 1963, one of a production line of youngsters who were brought to the club by that wonderful scout Charlie Ferguson. Charlie was responsible for unearthing some terrific footballing talent for Sunderland Football Club, particularly from north of the border, although it's doubtful whether he ever found a more talented youngster than Bobby Kerr.

Mind you, when I first clapped eyes on the wee lad, I have to confess to wondering just how such a slightly built youngster would cope with the physical demands of First Division football. In those days English football's top flight was a much tougher environment than the current game where the more skilful players are afforded much greater protection from referees.

Back in the 1960s just about every club had their own particular hard-men; Norman Hunter at Leeds United, Tommy Smith at Liverpool and Ron Harris at Chelsea to name but a few. These guys and others like them always made sure the more skilful and talented players were given something of a rough ride every time they ran out onto the park!

What I should have realised of course, was that real footballing talent will always shine through and there's no doubt Bobby had that in abundance. To say he exploded onto the first team scene is no exaggeration and after scoring a last-minute winner against Manchester City on his debut, he inspired the team to a great run in the FA Cup that saw us reach the 5th round and a mouth-watering tie against Leeds United at Roker Park. Sadly, tragedy struck in that game when Bobby was carried from the field with a broken leg after a challenge from Norman Hunter brought his early career in the game to a shuddering halt. Undeterred he fought back to fitness only to suffer another devastating blow when he broke the same leg again in a comeback game at Ashington a little over a year later.

Such misfortune would surely have dampened many a youngster's spirits but in typical fashion Bobby battled back to make it into the first team again, before eventually becoming our captain and of course leading us to that unforgettable triumph over Leeds United in the 1973 FA Cup Final. After football, Bobby has had more than his fair share of misfortune, not least when his wife Linda died suddenly leaving the wee man to bring up their eight-year-old son James. To his huge credit though, he stuck to the task with remarkable courage and he now has every right to be proud that James has grown up to become a fine young man.

I played alongside Bobby for virtually all his Sunderland career, the memories of which are captured wonderfully in this excellent publication and I'm proud to say that along with many of our former colleagues, we remain close friends to this day. Quite simply, the team spirit that existed when we played together during those wonderful days at Roker Park during the 1960s & 70s has never deserted us.

Jim Montgomery

It's over 40 years since Sunderland's incredible 1973 FA Cup win and even now, I still wonder at the magnitude of our achievements that season.

We produced what was widely acclaimed as the greatest giant-killing story in the entire history of the competition and when I climbed the steps to the Royal Box and lifted the FA Cup in front of the massed ranks of Sunderland fans, it was the fulfilment of a dream that a few short months earlier would have seemed utterly unthinkable.

Against all the odds, our new manager Bob Stokoe had transformed our ailing Second Division side into a team of world-beaters as we swept aside favourites Manchester City, Arsenal and finally Leeds United to lift what was then English football's most coveted prize.

For Bob it was the highlight of his managerial career and on Wearside he received acclaim of biblical proportions when he was named 'The Messiah' by Sunderland fans. We had achieved what many pundits felt was impossible and for months after the final the town of Sunderland was awash with celebrations.

But as the dust began to settle I couldn't help thinking of Bob's predecessor Alan Brown and the debt I owed to the man I regarded so highly. Had it not been for him my Sunderland career and the glory of 1973 simply would not have happened. No fewer than nine of the cup-winning team were players that he had developed and each and every one had absolute respect for the man. Brown was hard man, no question, and there were occasions when I really hated him but he knew how to run a football club that's for sure and speaking personally, I thought the world of him.

Alan Brown was a name synonymous with the early post-war era of Sunderland Football Club, a manager who was a tough disciplinarian and ruled the club with a rod of iron. His first steps into management came in August 1954 when he took over as Burnley boss, soon earning himself a reputation as an innovative coach and developer of young players. At Turf Moor he set up a scouting network that soon began to develop a production line of youngsters, many from the North East, who would ultimately bring the league championship and European football to the unfashionable Lancashire club.

By then however, Brown had moved on taking over as Sunderland boss in July 1957 after a brief spell coaching Sheffield Wednesday and he immediately made what many would later regard as one of the most significant appointments of Sunderland's early post-war history when he installed Charlie Ferguson as chief scout. Ferguson had worked for Brown at Burnley, helping to develop a youth policy that had developed some of the finest young players in the English game and in the almost three decades he served the club, he unearthed a wealth of talent, an almost never-ending list of players that would make it to the Sunderland first team, including no fewer than nine of the 1973 FA Cup-winning team, myself included.

Charlie hailed from Alexandria, the same Scottish town where I was born and brought up and spent much of his time scouring that particular part of the country for young footballing talent. I subsequently discovered that his mother still lived in the area so perhaps that was why he spent so much time up there, but for Sunderland Football Club it must have seemed like he was working

CHARLIE FERGUSON & BOB STOKOE

ALAN BROWN

MAM & DAD

The Kerr family didn't have much in the way of material things

but our parents instilled into us the importance of walking tall and doing good turns before bad and that is something that remains with the family to this day.

a goldmine as a procession of outstanding young players headed down to Roker Park. Charlie and my father had actually gone to school together and met by chance one day when Charlie was on his way to watch me play for the first time. He told my father he'd heard one or two good reports about a young lad called Bobby Kerr and had decided to check him out. You can imagine Charlie's reaction when my father told him it was actually his son he was referring to!

After that Charlie was a regular spectator at our games, keeping tabs on my progress and would often pop into our house for a chat. He told us all about Sunderland and the plans Alan Brown had for the club and it didn't take too long to convince me that Roker Park was the place for me. To be honest there was never any interest from other clubs and it was more or less accepted that when I was old enough I would be heading down to Wearside for trials.

To say there was sporting blood in the Kerr household is certainly no exaggeration, with my brothers George and Bill both having a real talent for the game and my sister Agnes going on to achieve national recognition as an accomplished hockey player. I've often wondered where we inherited this sporting prowess because as far as I can ascertain no one in our family history had any sort of involvement with sport although my uncle Robert had played in goal for Dumbarton in the 1930s. My father had little more than a passing interest in football although, as head of a protestant family he always had an allegiance to Rangers and in the tenement block where we lived, Saturday nights were particularly lively when, after a few drinks, he would switch on the record player and play 'The Sash My Father Wore' just to annoy our neighbour who supported Celtic. He in turn would respond by blasting out his Irish music and as the night drew on the music got louder and louder, much to the annoyance of our mother and just about everyone else in the building too!

The Kerr family didn't have much in the way of material things but our parents instilled into us the importance of walking tall and doing good turns before bad and that is something that remains with the family to this day. Our dad Bill worked as a clerk with Blackburns in Dumbarton and later for Singer Sewing Machines before taking up a part-time job in the local library when he retired. However, the boss in the household was our mother Mary, who really had her hands full keeping the six children Agnes, Billy, George, Margaret, Jean and myself in line!

My eldest brother Billy was a Scottish Youth international and played as an amateur for Queens Park however George was the first to break into the professional game when he headed south to join Barnsley and I've him to thank for my first set of football boots which arrived courtesy of the Yorkshire club. They were the old traditional style which were made of really thick leather and came right up around the ankle unlike the trim 'continental' style boots that were becoming the fashion in the late 1950s. Nevertheless, I treasured those boots and would clean them meticulously each week and then apply lashings of 'Dubbin' with its unique smell to waterproof and soften the leather.

LEVENVALE SCHOOL 1953 - THAT'S ME, FRONT ROW, SECOND FROM THE LEFT

THE KERR CLAN MEET AT A FAMILY WEDDING

MAM & DAD ON HOLIDAY

ON HOLIDAY IN ABERDEEN WITH JEAN & MARGARET CIRCA 1955

"Actually, most weeks I would get paid by the boys to clean the boots - what a task, and they insisted on them sparkling like a new pin! Mother and father were very proud of the family but more so the boys although father was their biggest critic even though he'd never kicked a ball in his life. Mother was at many a local football ground shouting them on while father shall we say, sometimes liked his whisky a little too much!

There's was never a lot of money in the family with mam and dad sometimes struggling to make ends meet having to bring up six kids and I remember on one occasion Bobby and I decided to embark on a small business venture to add a little money to the family coffers. The first thing we tried was selling firewood to the neighbours. We acquired scraps of wood from our grandad which Bobby sat and chopped into sticks and then tied them with wire just like the kindling that was sold in the shops. We managed to fill a whole barrow-load which we sold in no time and then raced home to eagerly await our mother coming in from work so we could hand over the money. Unfortunately we hadn't reckoned with her pride and we both ended up with a slap before being sent out to return the money and to make matters worse, we didn't even get the sticks back! Some time afterwards we tried a similar venture, this time selling bunches of flowers from our grandad's garden and again we got the same reaction from mam. She was an extremely proud woman and even though times were hard she didn't want anyone to think we were poor. Make no mistake, she was in charge of the Kerr household and even now whenever there's a thunderstorm we say: 'There's poor Will getting a row from Mary!"

Margaret Johnson (Bobby's sister).

LEVENVALE SCHOOL TEAM RUSSELL CUP-WINNERS 1959. I'M IN THE FRONT ROW, SECOND FROM THE LEFT

Like most young lads who grew up in the post-war austerity of 1950s Britain, I spent virtually all my spare time playing football. On my way to school in the morning, during break-time and till it was dark at night, all my pals and I ever wanted to do was kick the ball around. Even the weather wouldn't deter us and I remember during one particularly cold winter, the goalmouth in the public park where we played being frozen solid and I hit upon the idea of acquiring some salt.

Of course, none of us had any money so I nipped home and 'borrowed' a shilling from my mother's purse and headed around to the local general dealers to make the purchase. The plan seemed to have worked a treat until I headed home later that night to discover that my auntie had spotted me leaving the shop and had immediately told my mother. Needless to say, I was in real bother that night!

Another occasion I remember being in hot water was when Margaret and I had one hell of fight which started because I had refused to put coal on the fire, which was my job every night just before mam and dad came in from work. Margaret was cutting bread at the time and suddenly came after me with the knife. Fortunately, I managed to avoid her lunge by jumping over the settee but in doing so brought the light fitting crashing to the floor. It was one of these fancy three -way lights which my dad had just put up a few days earlier so yet again it was a slap and a lecture that went on most of the night!

Breaking into the school team was one of my fondest childhood memories and I'll never forget the excitement of playing in an organised game and wearing a football strip for the first time. You have to remember that the 1950s were hard times and most families simply didn't have the money to buy their sons such luxuries, in fact I'm pretty certain I was one of only a few who actually owned proper football boots!

My school was Levenvale Juniors and while they were generally happy days, I have to confess that football always took precedence over lessons and often to the point where I ended up in hot water, particularly when there was live international football on television! In those days floodlit football hadn't really taken off and international games were often played on a Wednesday afternoon, much to the liking of football daft youngsters such as me who relished a rare opportunity to see some of the world's top players in action.

Soon a regular pattern began to develop with a large number of male pupils strangely missing from lessons on certain Wednesday afternoons. Eventually the penny dropped with our teachers and we were hauled in front of the headmaster, although for one or two of us that initial dressing down didn't do the trick and eventually we were issued an ultimatum: 'Stop the Wednesday afternoon disappearances or you won't be playing in the school team again.' My real passion was always playing the game, particularly for the school so I really had no choice, even though I loved watching those televised games.

JIM BAXTER PICTURED AT FULHAM'S CRAVEN COTTAGE GROUND JUST AFTER HE'D JOINED SUNDERLAND

We had one or two excellent players in the school team including Drew Busby who almost followed me to Sunderland before eventually joining Third Lanark where holds the distinction of scoring the last ever goal for the club before they went out of existence in 1967. Drew and I played together throughout our school years and by the time we were 15 we were both turning out for Dumbarton Castle Rovers, the local under-18 team. In 1959, we both played in the Levenvale team that swept the board winning the league and lifting the coveted Russell Cup which was a major achievement for our school and I remember Hughie Gallacher, one of the star players at nearby Dumbarton at the time, coming along to present the trophies.

We were also rewarded with a trip to see Rangers play at Ibrox, an unbelievable treat for a group of football-daft youngsters who rarely, if ever, got the opportunity to visit the big city. I'll never forget the excitement as we boarded to train to Glasgow and then seeing Ibrox stadium for the first time. Before the game we were taken up to the famous 'Blue Room' and then into the trophy room where we could only stare in amazement at the amount of silverware on display. The biggest thrill of all came when we took our place on the terraces and the teams ran out onto the pitch to a massive roar from the 40-50,000 fans packed inside the ground. That was my first taste of big-time football, and I loved it!

As the game progressed, I found my attention being drawn to one of the Rangers players, a tall, slim midfielder who to me, even with my limited knowledge of the game, appeared to be running the show without even breaking sweat. As I watched throughout that first-half I lost count of the number of passes he made, each one delivered with pin-point accuracy. It was only at half-time when I checked my programme that I discovered that the player in question was Jim Baxter, a 20-year-old youngster who had just joined the club from Raith Rovers.

The next time I saw Jim Baxter play was on television three years later in a game against England that would earn the Rangers star legendary status for all time north of the border. By then 'Slim Jim', as he had become known, was already established in the Scotland team but on this particular afternoon at Wembley he destroyed 'The Auld Enemy', scoring both the goals in a 2-1 victory and producing a virtuoso performance that Scotland fans still enthuse over to this day. As I celebrated along with countless thousands of fellow countrymen that night, it would have been impossible to imagine that within a few short years I would be lining up alongside the great man in the English First Division!

It was only a few weeks after that famous Scotland victory in 1963 that I headed down to Wearside for the first time to meet Sunderland boss Alan Brown. I was accompanied by my father and Charlie Ferguson and for me, it was quite an adventure considering it was the first time I'd been south of the border, in fact I'd only ever been outside of Alexandria on a handful of occasions!

"Bobby and I grew up a few miles from each other and my earliest memory is of Bobby playing for Levenvale Primary School in a competition called the Russell Cup which was for primary schools in Dunbartonshire.

It was very well supported and the games were played at Milburn Park, home of Vale of Leven Juniors FC. Bobby's school had a decent team but the main attraction was the wee boy in the pink laces, Bobby Kerr, and people went along just to see him play such was his natural ability - he could dribble, pass, shoot and had a real football brain even at primary school age."

John O'Hare

JOHN O'HARE

GEORGE HERD

When we arrived at Roker Park, Charlie ushered us straight to a tiny room deep below the main stand terraces where I met another Scot who would have a massive influence on my career, Sunderland physio Johnny Watters.

Johnny was a marvellous character although when Charlie introduced us at that first meeting he was hardly complimentary about my lack of inches when, after eyeing me up and down for a few seconds, he asked: 'Has Alan Brown seen the size of him?' This was my first taste of Johnny's dry sense of humour which in the years ahead would often have the lads in stitches and for a number of us, keep us going while we were recovering from injury. He was a fantastic guy and I soon discovered that his tiny treatment room was the very heartbeat of Roker Park.

Alan Brown's office was a very different environment however and I have to confess to feeling slightly intimidated when I met the man for the first time. I can only liken it to being back at school and being wheeled in to see the headmaster for a dressing down. He lectured me on behaviour, discipline and hard work and stressed the importance of adhering to the dress code that prevailed at the club. Even though they were the height of fashion, jeans would not be tolerated and to this day I can honestly say I've never worn a pair. That was the mentality Alan Brown instilled in me, 'suited and booted' was always the order of the day. Similarly, you weren't allowed to have a beard or moustache although I did relent on that one soon after he'd left the club. That first meeting was brief and to the point and left me in no doubt that I needed to tow the line, or else!

Sunderland had booked us into the Roker Hotel situated on the sea front a few hundred yards from the ground, although for the two nights we were stayed there I was left with little or nothing to do as Charlie and my Dad went off to town for a few drinks. I ended up spending both nights sitting in reception chatting to the bellboy, cracking lad who I got to know pretty well in the years ahead as 'The Roker' was always our pre-match rendezvous during my time at Sunderland.

Like most young players living away from home in those days, I spent my first few years living in digs, in my case at 5 Hampden Road situated directly behind the Fulwell End of the ground. Here, I was looked after wonderfully well by our landlady Aggie Fenwick and from my very first day there, I immediately felt at home not least because fellow Scots George Herd and John O'Hare were also living there along with Irish winger Norman Clarke.

George was the senior player in the house, his status signified by a sparkling new, bright red Ford Capri parked at the door and also by the fact that he always got steaks for his evening meal while the rest of us had to settle for a more modest diet! Shortly after moving in, I made the mistake of telling Aggie that I happened to like banana sandwiches and after that it was always: 'I've got your favourite Bobby!'

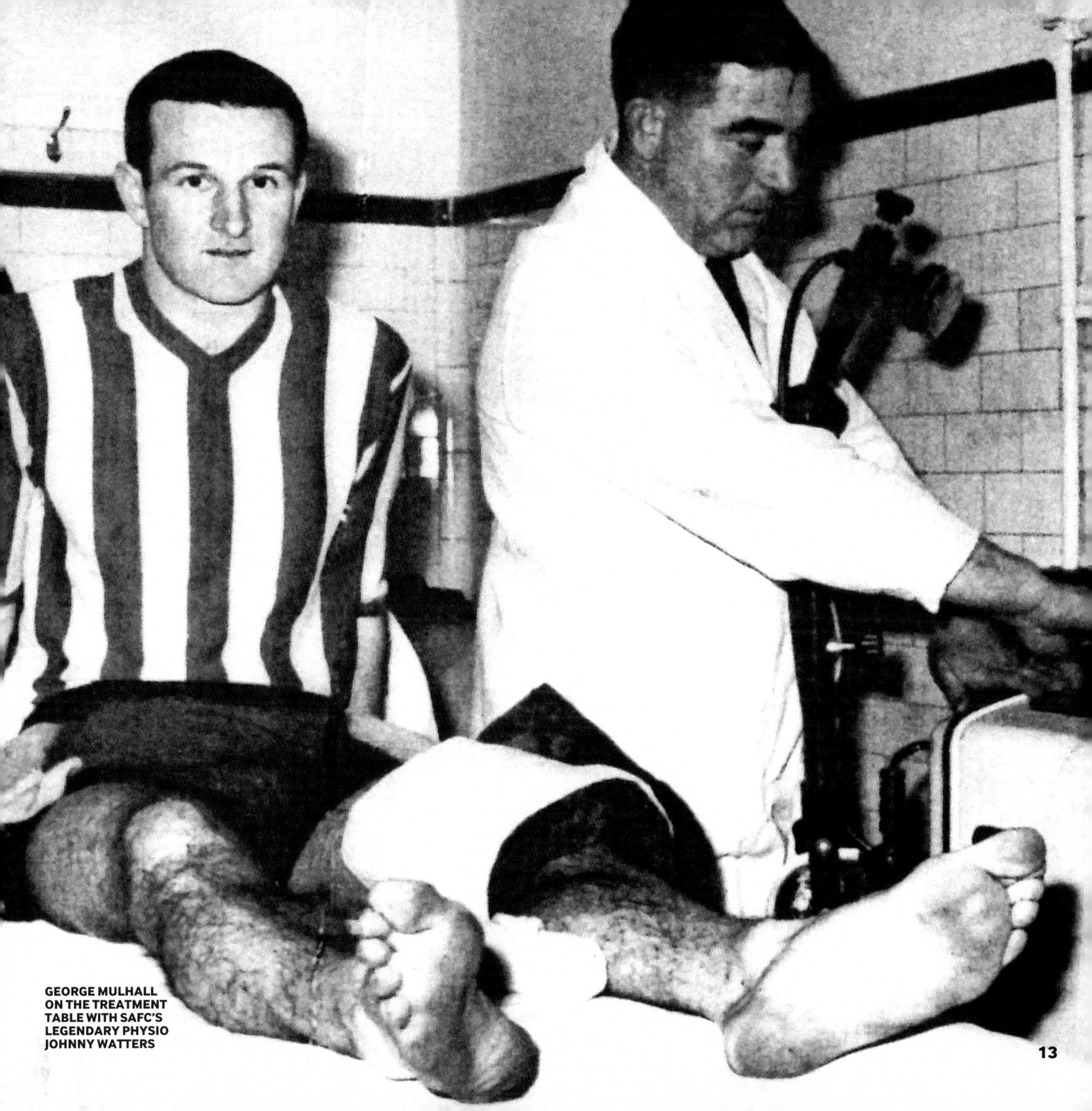

GEORGE MULHALL ON THE TREATMENT TABLE WITH SAFC'S LEGENDARY PHYSIO JOHNNY WATTERS

BRIAN CLOUGH WAS A PHENOMENAL GOAL SCORER AND HERE HE IS SCORING AGAINST NEWCASTLE UNITED IN THE TYNE-WEAR DERBY AT ST JAMES' PARK IN OCTOBER 1962

Years later I remember Gordon Strachan stating that his liking for bananas was the main reason he was able to play on so long at the top level. Well, if that was the case, I should be still playing now considering the number I ate in those days!

John O'Hare hailed from the same area of Scotland as I did and was another product of Charlie Ferguson's scouting prowess, in fact I followed John right through the ranks at Roker Park before we eventually became first-team colleagues. Norman Clarke was out injured when I first arrived at Hampden Road having torn his cruciate ligaments, which in those days was an injury from which few, if any, ever recovered. Sadly for Norman, who apparently was an outstanding left-winger who had just become established in the first team, he was forced to retire shortly afterwards.

"I joined Sunderland as a schoolboy at the start of the 1962-63 season being a year older than Bobby and it was midway through that season that I heard that Bobby was going to join me at Roker Park. I was in digs a 5 Hampden Road with Mr & Mrs Fenwick along with George Herd, Norman Clarke, Danny Hegan, and a lad from Nottingham, John McEvoy. At the end of the season Danny and John left and shortly afterwards Bobby arrived - I remember well him coming down with his Rangers scarf and with me being a Celtic man I wasted no time in giving him a bit of stick! But we got on really well and became close friends doing most things together, which in those days was mainly the bowling alley or Seaburn."

John O'Hare

Another player hobbling around Roker Park at that time was Brian Clough, who had also suffered the same career shattering injury in a game against Bury on Boxing Day 1962. I knew little about football south of the border but soon discovered that Clough was one of most prolific goalscorers in the English game and had averaged a goal a game throughout his career. Everyone knew he was desperate to get back and I can still see him now pounding up and down the Roker End terraces in a brave but ultimately forlorn attempt to regain fitness.

I had very little opportunity to play on the hallowed Roker Park turf in those early days as youth team games were always played on the police field at Hendon, pretty much where the Raich Carter Centre is located today. The man who looked after the youth team was Bill Scott, a wonderful character who had enjoyed a lengthy playing career at Preston North End and literally lived and breathed football. Alan Brown was a regular visitor to our games, although invariably standing alone on the touchline making notes and other than the few occasional words of advice, he kept himself in the background.

We played in the Northern Intermediate League and regularly came up against many up and coming youngsters who would go on to make a name for themselves at the top level. One in particular was Eddie Gray of Leeds United, a left-winger with a wonderful talent and we had one or two terrific battles in those youth team games. Almost ten years later would come the ultimate confrontation of course, when we came face to face again in the FA Cup final at Wembley.

"I used to watch Bobby playing for the youth team and it was pretty obvious he was a young talent that was certain to make the grade in top class football. I remember when he first came down he used to get really annoyed when I was on best steak for my evening meal when he and the rest of the lads were on scrambled eggs and such like and I remember telling him: 'Listen Bobby, one day you might be lucky enough to get into the first team - then you'll get steak!"

George Herd

GEORGE HERD PICTURED OUTSIDE OUR DIGS IN HAMPDEN ROAD

"When I arrived at Sunderland the club put me up in the somewhat luxurious surroundings of the Roker Hotel so when I moved to Hampden Road it was something of a culture shock! When Bobby arrived we couldn't believe how small he was and John and I used to wind him up mercilessly about his size but he was a great little lad and took it all in good part. One of the regular meals on 'Ma' Fenwick's menu was mince, mashed potato and brussel sprouts and it appeared that Bobby had never had sprouts before when he commented: 'These little cabbages are nice!'

To be honest, 'Ma' Fenwick's fare was pretty dire but fortunately, a native of my home town lived in Spelterworks Road on the south side of the town and I used to take the lads across there every few weeks for a good old fry up! Mrs Fenwick had a niece, a very attractive girl, who would often come to help with the housework and one day she said to me: 'If I could bottle Bobby, I would make a fortune!' Bobby was starting to make a bit of a reputation for himself at the time and she was convinced he was going to be a big star! Of course, apart from football our main interest was girls and I remember when Valentine's Day approached in 1964 John, Bobby and I had a little bet as to who would receive the most cards. With John on the verge of the first team and Bobby starring in the youth team I was rank outsider being on my way out at Roker at the time. Anyway, I made sure the postman was alerted well in advance and when Valentine's Day came, John and Bobby both received seven cards but to their utter disbelief, I received eight!"

Norman Clarke

The bitter rivalry with Leeds United which followed me throughout my Roker Park career had apparently stemmed from a game at Elland Road in August 1962 when Sunderland inside-forward Willie McPheat had sustained a broken leg following what his colleagues described as a disgraceful challenge by Leeds United's Bobby Collins. Collins, at 5ft 4 inches tall, was no bigger than me but whereas I always avoided the rough stuff, the tiny Scottish international it seemed, wasn't afraid to put the foot in and on this occasion he had completely shattered the giant Sunderland forward's leg, an injury which ultimately ended his Roker Park career.

This controversial incident was just one of many which stemmed from the style of play manager Don Revie had instilled into the Yorkshire club as they quickly earned the reputation as the dirtiest team in the land. At the time Leeds, like Sunderland, were in the Second Division and as the 1963-64 season got under way it soon became apparent that the two clubs would become locked in a bitter battle in the promotion stakes.

The big show-down came when the teams met twice over the Christmas period, the first game at Elland Road on Boxing Day ending with honours even following a 1-1 draw. The return at Roker a few days later was one of the toughest games I've ever seen either before or since with tackles flying in from both sides right from the kick-off. If Leeds had come with the reputation as football's hardest team, then they were more than matched that afternoon, culminating in their striker Jim Storrie being carried from the pitch midway through the second half. Sunderland won the game 2-0, but I remember sitting up in the stands thinking to myself: 'If this is English football then maybe I should start and think about another career!'

There were over 55,000 inside Roker that afternoon but that was nothing compared to the crowds that descended on the ground one Wednesday night a few months later. The first team were having a fantastic season and, apart from chasing promotion they were also enjoying a great run in the FA Cup. In the fifth round they had beaten reigning English League champions Everton to set up a mouth-watering tie against Manchester United at Old Trafford. Although, I didn't travel down to Manchester, by all accounts the game was a classic and one that Sunderland should have won when they were leading 3-1 with only minutes to go only for Matt Busby's side to save the day with two late goals.

The return leg at Roker Park a few days later created massive interest on Wearside but few could have predicted the scenes that developed outside the ground as kick-off time approached. My normal routine was to head around to the ground an hour or so before kick-off but when I opened the front door of our digs in Hampden Road, I was immediately confronted by a sea of people packed across the full width of the road to the point where I was struggling to even get out of the front gate. In the end it took me almost an hour to force my way through the crowds to the players' entrance only a few hundred yards away, and I arrived just in time to see the game start!

CHARLIE HURLEY REASSURES JIM MONTGOMERY AFTER THE SUNDERLAND KEEPER HAD BEEN INJURED FOLLOWING A LATE CHALLENGE FROM LEEDS UNITED'S CENTRE-FORWARD IAN LAWSON DURING THE 1963 PROMOTION BATTLE AT ROKER PARK

CHARLIE HURLEY IS CHAIRED AROUND ROKER PARK AFTER A 2-1 VICTORY OVER CHARLTON ATHLETIC IN THE FINAL HOME GAME OF THE SEASON HAD CLINCHED PROMOTION BACK TO THE TOP FLIGHT. L TO R: JOHNNY CROSSAN, CEC IRWIN, CHARLIE HURLEY, JIMMY McNAB, LEN ASHURST, JIM MONTGOMERY & GEORGE MULHALL

The scenes inside the ground were almost as bad with St John's Ambulance men working overtime to tend the injured fans. Then the word filtered through that one of the main exit gates at the Roker End had collapsed under the sheer weight of numbers allowing thousands of fans to pour into the ground. Goodness knows how many people were actually inside the ground that night and had there been perimeter fences around the terraces we would surely have been witnessing a disaster of Hillsborough proportions. Fortunately, many fans were able to escape the packed terraces by climbing onto the running track and when the game got under way there were hundreds sitting right up to the touchline. Amazingly the game had started on time and again it was a terrific match which Sunderland should have won after twice being in front but in the end they had to settle for a 2-2 draw after extra-time.

The following morning it was very much the calm after the storm but as I walked around to the players' entrance for training, the damage to the ground and surrounding property was there for all to see. However, the most amazing thing I can remember were the piles of lost shoes which the groundstaff had collected from the terraces and adjacent streets, there were literally hundreds stacked up against the wall under the main stand!

Although we were soundly beaten in the replay, promotion was never in doubt and there were huge celebrations at the end of the final home game of the season against Charlton Athletic after a 2-1 victory had clinched the club's place back in the top flight. Of course, I was just a youngster watching from the wings and to be honest I was in awe of the first team players, particularly captain Charlie Hurley who was a giant of a man in every sense of the word.

The fans had given him the nickname 'The King' and looking back, I have to agree because I don't think I played with a better all round player than Charlie. Apart from being probably the best centre-half in Britain at the time, he was also a true gentleman who always had time for the younger players at the club. He was also a great ambassador for Sunderland Football Club regularly doing work for various charities and visiting local hospitals.

As the club's long awaited return to Division One approached there was an air of optimism among supporters as season ticket sales hit record levels. Everything it seemed was geared up for a serious assault on the big league when suddenly the news broke that Alan Brown was leaving the club. Players and supporters alike were stunned. A few days later he was unveiled as Sheffield Wednesday's new boss while back on Wearside everyone was left to speculate on why the man who rebuilt the club so successfully had left when they were on the brink of the big time. In typical fashion, there was no positive reason coming from within the club and Brown, a very private man, remained tight-lipped. As a youth team player, I had no inkling of the politics going on behind the scenes but even the players who were closest to their manager had no idea why he had decided to leave the club so suddenly.

UNBELIEVABLE CROWD SCENES FROM THE FA CUP SIXTH ROUND REPLAY AGAINST MANCHESTER UNITED AT ROKER PARK.

BRIAN CLOUGH IN TYPICAL POSE

As my good friend Jimmy McNab later told me, it had come as a complete shock to everyone and none of the first team squad had even the slightest hint that he was contemplating packing in. Apparently, on the day the news broke Jimmy had been at home packing his car ready to head up to Scotland for a short break when Brown rang and told him to get over to his house straight away to sign a new contract he'd just agreed with the board. When Jim suggested that it would wait until after he returned, Brown insisted that he signed there and then so he delayed his journey for an hour or so, headed over to the boss' house in Cleadon and signed the contract. It was only when Jimmy arrived in Scotland later that day that he heard the news Alan Brown left the club. But that was typical of 'The Bomber', no one every got close to him and he never did reveal the true reason for his departure. However it was later rumoured that having secured new contracts for the players, he then approached the board for improved terms for himself and when they refused he resigned on a matter of principle.

With the man who had masterminded Sunderland's promotion success now gone it was hardly surprising that the team struggled to come to terms with the rigours of first division football. George Hardwick, the former Middlesbrough and England full-back, was eventually appointed as Brown's successor and, to his credit, managed to stabilise the club and relegation was avoided comfortably. From my point of view, the most significant change Hardwick made when he arrived at the club was to appoint Brian Clough as youth team manager. Clough had failed in his attempt at a comeback, playing only three games in the first team and netting his only goal in the top flight ironically against Leeds United, before being forced to call it a day. However, his appointment came as something of a surprise to most of us as it was common knowledge within Roker Park that the outspoken striker was less than popular in boardroom circles.

Even in those days, the arrogance that was to become his trademark in later years was there in abundance although there was little else to suggest he would go on to become one of the greatest managers in the history of English football. Everyone knew how badly he missed playing the game, particularly scoring goals and often our training sessions would consist of little more than getting balls into the box for Cloughie to blast them into the net!

As youth team manager he was pretty much 'jack of all trades' which among other things included running onto the pitch to tend to injured players. This was clearly something of a dent to the ego of a man who not long before had a reputation as one of the greatest goalscorers in the game receiving the adulation of the crowd every time he stepped out onto the pitch. Before every game he would remind us: 'If you go down injured, make sure you are bloody injured, because I'm not running onto the pitch for nothing!'

SUNDERLAND YOUTH TEAM 1964-65

JIMMY McNAB

GEORGE HARDWICK

JIM BAXTER AND HIS WIFE JEANNIE ARRIVE AT THE ROKER HOTEL JUST BEFORE THE LEGENDARY SCOTTISH INTERNATIONAL JOINED SUNDERLAND IN A £72,000 TRANSFER FROM RANGERS

Nevertheless, I think Cloughie relished the job and results did suggest the former striker might just have something of a talent for management as we reached the semi-finals of the FA Youth Cup before eventually losing to Everton. In fairness, he had inherited a decent squad of players including goalkeeper Derek Forster and John O'Hare who had already broken into the first team and then there were the likes Colin Todd and Colin Suggett who both went on to have great careers in football.

One player who also appeared on the scene that season was Billy Hughes, another Scot unearthed by Charlie Ferguson who would also go on to have a great career in the game. Billy and I immediately became great pals although I suspect Cloughie wasn't too impressed with our antics at times and I remember at the end of one training session he called us over and instructed us to wash George Hardwick's car. Billy and I had a few quiet words and agreed we were having none of it and told him so in no uncertain terms: 'Look, we're here to play football, not to wash cars!'

As you might imagine, Clough was furious but as we walked off the pitch a few minutes later, he approached us again: 'Look, I agree you're both here to play football, but if you would do this for me on this occasion, I promise I won't ask you again.' It was a compromise and we ended up washing the manager's car, albeit somewhat reluctantly. In fairness to Clough he never did ask us again so I suppose we'd won the moral victory although I shudder to think how he would have reacted a few years later if any of his youth team players at Derby or Forest had refused to obey his orders!

Brian Clough's reign as youth team manager at Roker was short lived however when, at the end of the 1964-65 season, he and manager George Hardwick were shown the door. Hardwick's departure was somewhat surprising bearing in mind the improvements he'd brought in terms of first team results and I later heard that he'd also wanted to promote Clough to assistant manager. There were politics flying around the Roker Park boardroom at the time and it was common knowledge that the directors wanted Clough out of the club even though Hardwick had apparently spotted the former striker's managerial potential. It was a decision that would haunt the Sunderland hierarchy for years as they watched Clough climb to the very top of the managerial tree lifting numerous domestic and European honours along the way.

If a wind of change had blown through the corridors of Roker Park during the 1964-65 season, then the following campaign saw nothing less than the beginning of a full-scale revolution at the club! It began with the appointment of former Scotland boss Ian McColl as manager but perhaps more importantly, it was his first foray into the transfer market and the signing of none other than my boyhood idol Jim Baxter that would ultimately throw the Roker Park dressing room into absolute turmoil.

IAN McCOLL

My initial reaction to Jim's arrival at the club was one of utter disbelief and I simply couldn't believe that I would be training alongside the man who I had idolised for so long from the Ibrox terraces. Baxter had established himself as arguably the best left-sided midfield player in the game, signified by the fact that he was selected to play for the Rest of the World against England at Wembley in 1963 and for Sunderland he was a massive coup when you consider they had apparently beaten off competition from the likes of Liverpool and Manchester United.

Unfortunately it was pretty obvious from day one that the club's new signing was about to become a disruptive influence in the Roker Park dressing room and we soon discovered that Slim Jim found gambling and alcohol infinitely more attractive than the rigid day to day discipline that Alan Brown had demanded from his players. Charlie Hurley was still very much the club's star player but when Baxter announced that there wasn't enough room for two 'Kings' at the club, it was pretty obvious that the two players were on a collision course.

Speaking personally, I found Jim to be a smashing guy and even though I hadn't broken into the first team at that point, he would often sit and chat to me with no hint of his superstar status. However, I'm sure the established first team players would tell a different story and even just watching from the sidelines it was clear to see the togetherness and unity that Alan Brown had instilled in the club literally falling apart at the seams.

Ian McColl seemed either unable or unwilling to tackle the situation which was visibly wrecking morale in the dressing room and as Baxter's first season progressed it gradually became apparent that the wayward Scot had a massive influence over his former boss. In fact, it was even suggested that Jim was picking the team and this was reinforced with the signing of his cousin George Kinnell, a rugged central defender who was immediately handed Charlie Hurley's coveted number 5 shirt. It must have been a heartbreaking time for Charlie who for so long had been the top man at the club and now found himself relegated to the reserves.

New Years Eve 1966 will always live long in my memory for that was the day I made my debut in the Sunderland first team although, even in my wildest dreams I couldn't have imaged a more dramatic introduction to top-class football! I'd been on the fringe of the first team for a number of weeks and had joined the squad at the Roker Hotel for our pre-match lunch with no thoughts of actually being involved in the forthcoming game against Manchester City. A couple of hours before kick-off we'd set off on the short walk to Roker Park when Baxter put his arm around me, bent over and whispered: 'Listen Bobby, George Herd's just failed a fitness test so you're playing this afternoon.'

JIM BAXTER'S COUSIN GEORGE KINNELL WITH AUTOGRAPH HUNTERS OUTSIDE ROKER PARK SHORTLY AFTER JOINING SUNDERLAND FROM OLDHAM ATHLETIC

JOHN O'HARE IN ACTION AGAINST CHELSEA AT ROKER PARK. JOHN WAS ONE OF THE BEST YOUNG PROSPECTS AT THE CLUB AND ALWAYS HAD AN EYE FOR GOAL

My initial reaction was one of panic but there was little time for nerves and I was soon in the dressing room getting ready to walk out onto Roker Park for the biggest day of my life. Whether telling me so late had been a deliberate ploy to prevent my pre-match nerves I'm not sure, but the fact that it was Jim who broke the news to me did seem to confirm the rumours of his ever-increasing involvement in team selection matters!

As for the game itself, I can't remember too much other than the amazing finale that unfolded in the dying minutes. McColl had told me to stay out on the right wing and get crosses in at every opportunity and in the opening stages I remember racing up and down the touchline frantically looking over my shoulder for the pass that would set me away.

After the first few attacks Baxter came over and said: 'Look Bobby, there's no need to keep looking for the ball - just you get down the wing and it will arrive!' And sure enough it did, with amazing regularity and with such a degree of accuracy that I didn't even need to check my stride. But that was Baxter, the finest passer of a ball I ever came across in the game.

Overall, I think I faired pretty well during my first appearance on the English First Division stage but the game itself was a dour encounter and seemed to be heading for a goal-less draw when, with only a couple of minutes remaining, I was presented with a chance at the Fulwell End of the ground. I'm not sure who played the ball through and to be honest it wasn't the sweetest shot I'd ever hit but when it ended up in the net, the ground erupted as I was soon buried under my celebrating team-mates. Moments later the final whistle blew and as we trooped into the dressing room I'm certain there can't have been a happier man in English football on that particular afternoon.

By good fortune, my father was there to witness the game having driven down to Wearside to give John O'Hare and I a lift back home to Alexandria for the Hogmanay celebrations. Of course, when he set off he hadn't banked on seeing me make my debut let alone score the winner so there was extra cause for celebration that night and when we arrived home we found that the whole family together with friends and neighbours had converged on the Kerr household to hail the return of the prodigal son. Apparently, the celebrations continued well into the early hours although I have little recollection other than waking up mid-afternoon on New Year's Day with a throbbing headache. Remember, I was only seventeen at the time and had barely taken a drink before that night other than the odd glass of beer. My introduction to spirits and whisky in particular began that fateful night and as I was soon to learn in the months and years ahead, they were almost be a prerequisite if you intended to rub shoulders socially with the Roker Park first-team set.

'SLIM JIM'

My performance in the City game had obviously impressed Ian McColl and I retained my place for our next game at Blackpool where George Herd came off the bench to earn us a point in a 1-1 draw. The following week we came up against a strong Chelsea side at Roker but beat them comfortably 2-0.

Again I managed to find the target but this time I have to say it was cracking finish, a volley from the edge of the box that gave England 'keeper Peter Bonetti no chance.

Of all the goals I went on to score in top-class football, I still rate that one as the best.

NEIL MARTIN WAS BRILLIANT IN THE AIR. THIS IS THE FIRST OF HIS TWO GOALS IN A 4-1 VICTORY OVER SHEFFIELD UNITED AT ROKER PARK DURING THE 1966-67 SEASON

The team were now hitting a rich vein of form and the press were making a big thing about this 'Wonderkid' who was inspiring Sunderland's change in fortune. Certainly things were going well for me but it was pure chance that the turnaround in results had coincided with my arrival in the team. Looking back, I find it hard to believe that the team had struggled so badly given the vast array of talent at the club.

Apart from Baxter we had the likes Jim Montgomery, in my view the best keeper in the country next to Gordon Banks, internationals Martin Harvey, George Herd, George Mulhall and Neil Martin, one of the best headers of a ball I ever came across in the game. Another player who had broken into the first team that season was Colin Todd who was about to develop into one of the finest talents the club had ever produced although, sadly for Sunderland fans, Toddy's achievements in the game would ultimately be away from Roker Park.

The week after the Chelsea game we travelled to high-flying Leicester, a tough away fixture at any time and although we were a goal down at half-time, George Mulhall and John O'Hare secured the points for us with two second-half strikes. I'll always remember Baxter playing 'keepie-up' and basically 'taking the mickey' out of the City players as the game entered the closing stages. The wayward Scot's antics went down none too well with Matt Gillies, the City boss, who approached Baxter as we trooped off the pitch and gave him a piece of his mind only for Jim to annoy him even further with a typical broad grin of satisfaction!

As our unbeaten run continued it seemed I could do no wrong which was typified when I scored the opening goal in a 2-2 draw with Liverpool at Roker Park. I'd hit a speculative shot from the edge of the box which was straight at Liverpool 'keeper Tommy Lawrence who inexplicably failed to get his body behind the ball and then allowed it to slip from his grasp and over the line!

This was the game that my best mate Billy Hughes made his first-team debut and I also recall John O'Hare getting knocked unconscious when he headed our equaliser mid-way through the second-half. John was a fantastic front man and brave as a lion but he was another who would soon be allowed to leave Roker when he joined the Brian Clough revolution at Derby County. John would go on to win just about every honour in the game under Cloughie much to the annoyance of Sunderland fans who yet again had seen another talented youngster leave the club. Even more annoying perhaps was the fact that the fee received for his move to the Baseball Ground brought no more than £20,000 into the Roker coffers!

Without doubt, the biggest home game of the season was against arch rivals Newcastle United and I have to confess, I'd never experienced anything like the atmosphere inside Roker Park when I ran out onto the park for my first taste of a Tyne-Wear derby.

The bitter rivalry between supporters for these games often borders on pure hatred, so desperate are they to put one over on the enemy.

Fortunately, we were able to send our fans home happy with an emphatic 3-0 victory and the game was particularly memorable for me personally having netted two goals and in fact, I could have gone home with the match ball that night had a third goal not been chalked off following a dubious offside decision by the linesman!

ONE OF MY GOALS AGAINST 'THE MAGS'. A GLANCING HEADER THAT LEFT GOALKEEPER GORDON MARSHALL AND DEFENDER FRANK CLARK HELPLESS!

Our league form had seen us climb to a comfortable mid-table position and in the FA Cup we'd made it through to the fifth round after resounding victories over Brentford and Peterborough at Roker Park.

ON THE ATTACK DURING OUR 7-1 VICTORY OVER PETERBOROUGH UNITED IN THE FA CUP FOURTH ROUND AT ROKER PARK

GEORGE MULHALL AT LOGGERHEADS WITH THE LEEDS UNITED PLAYERS DURING THE FA CUP FIFTH ROUND TIE AT ROKER PARK

The draw favoured us with another home tie against none other than Leeds United, our bitter rivals from our Second Division days, who had gone from strength to strength following their promotion with Sunderland a few years earlier. Under Don Revie the Yorkshire side had established themselves as league title rivals alongside the likes of Liverpool and Manchester United and had also reached the FA Cup final in their first season back in the top flight in 1965.

Whilst Revie's team included many fine players they also had one or two hard-men and still carried the reputation as the most brutal team in the English game. Billy Bremner and Norman 'bites your legs' Hunter were the two players who seemed to be always hitting the headlines for their intimidating style of the play but the player I was told to watch out for was Johnny Giles, their talented Republic of Ireland international midfielder who allegedly also had something of a reputation in the game for producing shall we say, somewhat dubious tackles that would leave opponents writhing in agony!

Predictably, the tie generated enormous interest on Wearside and our fine form had prompted many pundits to install us as favourites to progress to the quarter-finals. Certainly confidence was high in our dressing room as we prepared for the biggest game of the season so far and for me personally, I somewhat naively looked upon the game as just another chapter in the Bobby Kerr success story. Up to that point everything I had touched seemed to have turned to gold and I saw no reason why the Leeds United game should be any different - how wrong can you be!

The incident that would turn my early career in professional football upside down came midway through the second-half when I chased the ball on the main stand touchline.

The ball was going out of play and experience would have taught me to leave it and take the throw-in but instead I made a desperate attempt to keep the ball in play and in doing so, set myself up as a target for a shuddering tackle from Norman Hunter. As soon as our shins met I heard the crack and even though I managed to hobble to the touchline, I knew I was in serious trouble.

Whether Hunter meant it or not, only he can say and predictably the press made a big thing about the tackle the following morning but in fairness to Norman, I couldn't honestly say it was deliberate.

As soon as I was lifted onto the treatment table Johnny Watters needed only one look to confirm that my right leg was broken and in no time at all I was in an ambulance heading for Monkwearmouth Hospital where Dr Scott, their consultant orthopaedic surgeon and also our club doctor carried out the operation to put the bone back in place.

RECOVERING IN HOSPITAL WITH EVERY BOY'S FAVOURITE IN THOSE DAYS, CHARLES BUCHAN'S SOCCER GIFT BOOK

WATCHING FROM THE ROKER PARK TUNNEL WITH MY RIGHT LEG IN PLASTER

The first man to come in to see me that night was Jim Baxter who was able to give me chapter and verse on the game which had ended in a 1-1 draw. Regardless of the unpopular image he had created with many of his teammates, there was another side to Slim Jim which few people saw and this was typical of the man. Little did I realise it at the time, but I would never play alongside the great man again.

The prognosis for recovery was good and I was told that all being well I would be back in action within six months although, as things turned out it would be another eighteen months before I pulled on a first-team shirt again. After leaving hospital I was looked after by my girlfriend Cathy's folks who lived in Canon Cockin Street in Grangetown. Cathy and I had met at the Locarno when John O'Hare and I were in there one night although not being interested in football, she hadn't a clue who we were and actually got John and I mixed up, so for most of that first night Cathy thought I was John O'Hare! Her folks were brilliant with me but I did have a lot of spare time on my hands during the day and once I was mobile I would often wander down to the nearby Commercial Road Working Mens' Club where the highlight of the week in those days was Sunday lunchtime strippers!

Another port of call in those days was The Regale in Hendon where I would fill in my time playing cards and dominoes with the locals. At the time I was only drinking Coke or Lemonade but my visits almost landed me in hot water with Ian McColl when a supporter wrote to the club complaining I was in there all day drinking. McColl called me into his office and started giving me a right dressing down but when I protested my innocence he seemed to accept my side of the story. That was the only time anyone ever complained to the club about my drinking habits, a little ironic perhaps given that I would soon join the drink culture that seemed almost obligatory in top-class football in those days!

My rehabilitation took place under the watchful eye of Johnny Watters and whilst I'd known for some time that he was a bit of a character, it was only now that I was able to experience first hand the wit and humour of one of the funniest men I ever had the pleasure to work with in football. Johnny had actually been a decent footballer in his younger days when he played for Celtic whilst studying at Glasgow University and he needed no encouragement to remind everyone that he had played in the Old Firm derby in 1939 which attracted a British record crowd of 118,000 to Ibrox!

Over the years Johnny had looked after countless great players including of course, Brian Clough whose career came to a shattering end when he tore his cruciate ligaments after colliding with Bury goalkeeper Chris Harker in a top-of-the-table promotion battle on Boxing Day 1962.

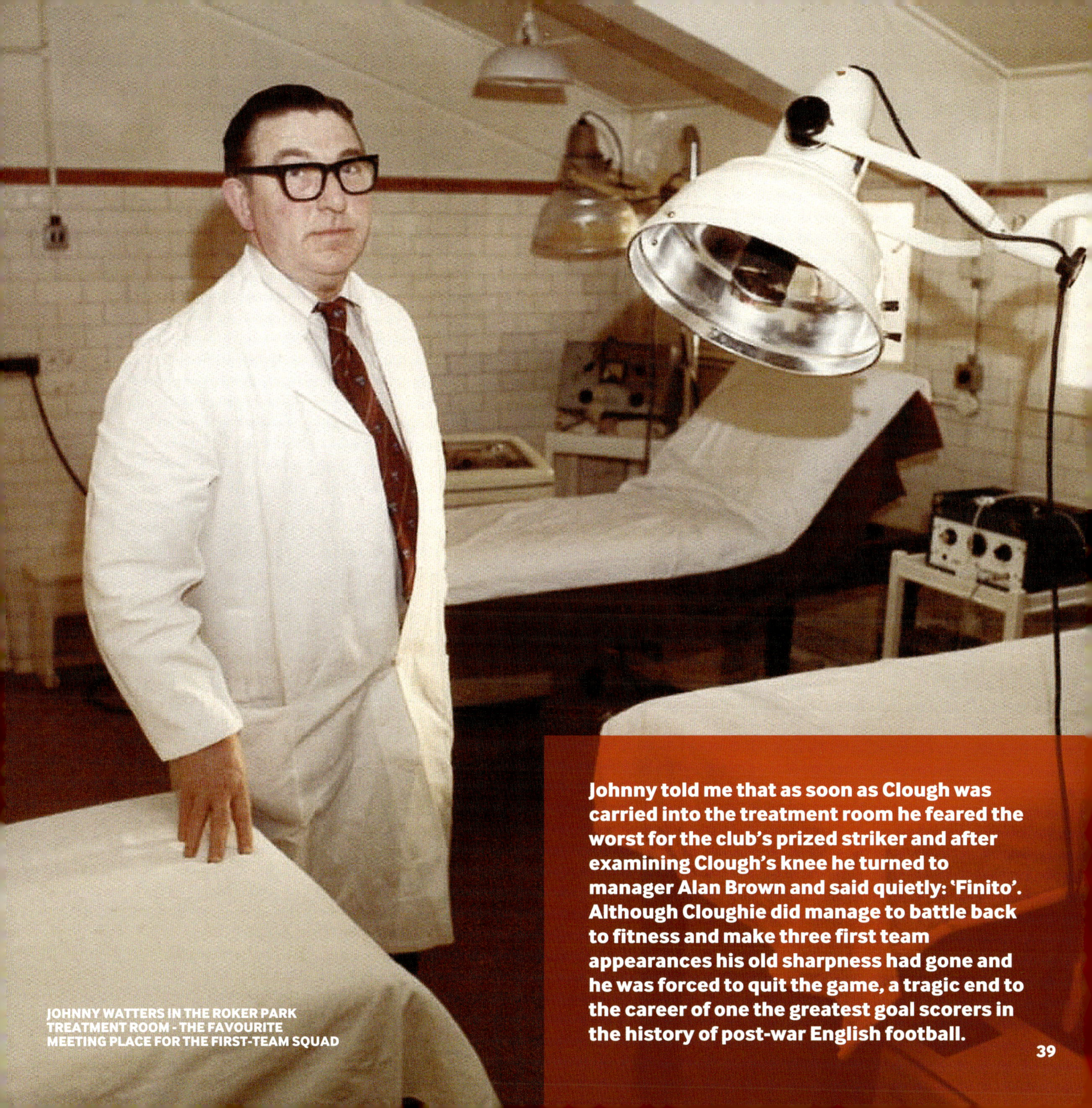

JOHNNY WATTERS IN THE ROKER PARK TREATMENT ROOM - THE FAVOURITE MEETING PLACE FOR THE FIRST-TEAM SQUAD

Johnny told me that as soon as Clough was carried into the treatment room he feared the worst for the club's prized striker and after examining Clough's knee he turned to manager Alan Brown and said quietly: 'Finito'. Although Cloughie did manage to battle back to fitness and make three first team appearances his old sharpness had gone and he was forced to quit the game, a tragic end to the career of one the greatest goal scorers in the history of post-war English football.

THE LEGENDARY RUSSIAN GOALKEEPER LEV YASHIN IN ACTION DURING HIS COUNTRY'S WORLD CUP QUARTER-FINAL TIE AGAINST HUNGARY IN 1966

In 1966 the World Cup came to England and Roker Park was chosen to host some of the games in the earlier rounds and it was during this period that Johnny was called on to look after some of the World's greatest players. One of the countries based on Wearside were Russia and after one of their games at Roker, their legendary goalkeeper Lev Yashin was selected to give a urine sample. Unfortunately, the giant 'keeper was struggling to produce the necessary liquid when someone suggested they should send for Johnny who could: 'Take the piss out of anybody.' Sure enough, Johnny entered the room and a few minutes later emerged with the required sample although no one ever did discover how he managed to get it!

Johnny's healing hands weren't restricted to footballers and he always had a number of private clients who would show their gratitude with a bottle of whisky or a joint of meat although he would never accept money as payment. However, even they weren't immune to Johnny's wicked sense of humour and on one occasion he had a patient lapping the pitch and doing various exercises as he bellowed out instructions from the directors' box. All the lads watching from the stand were in stitches as the poor chap responded to every command and he was almost on his knees as he left the ground probably never to return!

On another occasion, Jim Montgomery turned up one Sunday morning for treatment only to be told he'd have to wait outside as Johnny was busy with a private patient. It was only when that door opened that Monty discovered that the private patient was actually a greyhound!

As a physiotherapist, Johnny was regarded as one of the best in the business but when the conversation got into full flow he wouldn't always concentrate fully on the job in hand, as another private patient once discovered to his cost. The guy had complained of a problem with his ankle and after diagnosing a sprain Johnny said he would need to apply strapping but before doing so he would need to shave the leg. Johnny had just acquired some of the new Bic disposable razors and set about shaving the chap's left leg although none too expertly unfortunately as blood began to spurt everywhere. He then told the guy to turn over and then proceeded to shave the back of the right leg again with the same bloody results. Undeterred, Johnny duly applied the strapping to the left ankle and told him to come back a week later. Strangely, he never did return!

Apart from Johnny, the other man charged with looking after the players' fitness at Roker Park was Dr. Scott, a larger than life character whose step-son James Bolam went on to achieve fame on numerous television programmes including The Likely Lads and more recently, New Tricks. Dr. Scott and Johnny were great pals and both were great conversationalists although when they were together they'd often have a discussion going with each talking about a totally different subject! Every Friday the pair would head off to Edward Thompson's, a local printers owned by Frank Cronin, one of the club's director's, where they would have fish and chips in the staff canteen.

JIM BAXTER SLOTS HOME FROM THE SPOT DURING OUR 5-2 VICTORY OVER BRENTFORD IN THE FA CUP THIRD ROUND TIE AT ROKER PARK

SUNDERLAND DEFEND IN DEPTH AGAINST LEEDS UNITED DURING THE FIFTH ROUND REPLAY AT ELLAND ROAD

The problem was, eating a meal wouldn't deter either from speaking and often the food was flying in all directions. When they returned to the ground in the afternoon you only needed to look at their ties to see where they'd been - we used to call them 'canteen medals'!

Johnny's infectious humour certainly helped keep my spirits up and the road back to fitness developed into something of a long haul. The Leeds United game seemed a million miles away and it was frustrating to have to sit in the sidelines and watch the season that had promised so much turn into a one of bitter disappointment. The tie against the Yorkshire side had gone to a second replay which was played at Hull City's Boothferry Park ground with Don Revie's side winning 2-1, the decisive goal coming from a controversial late penalty. To make matters worse, George Herd and George Mulhall were sent off for protesting what appeared to be one of many questionable decisions that seemed to be associated with Leeds United in those days.

After that defeat results took a downturn and by the end of the campaign Sunderland finished in a disappointing 17th place in Division One.

The following season saw Jim Baxter's reign at Roker Park come to an end, much to the relief of many of his colleagues at Roker Park I suspect. His lifestyle had certainly taken its toll on his ability to produce the goods on the park and his physical appearance now bore little resemblance to the man who was once known as 'Slim Jim'. By now, Ian McColl had little control over his wayward star and must have inwardly regretted the day he ever signed Baxter who would regularly turn up for training after a night on the town and simply refuse partake in anything physical.

I remember on one occasion I was in the treatment room when the door opened and Jim threw his car keys to Johnny Watters saying: 'There's some money in the boot of my car Johnny, can you take care of it for me?' When Johnny went out to the car he discovered the boot literally full of notes, obviously the product of a successful night for Jim at one of the local casinos!

Whilst his performances on the park rarely hit the heights, Jim was still capable of producing the odd outstanding performance and one such game against Nottingham Forest effectively set up his move away from Roker Park. That afternoon Baxter was back to his brilliant best and so impressed was Forest boss Johnny Carey that he persuaded his club to part with £100,000 a few weeks later to secure the services of 'Slim Jim'. For Sunderland it was a great piece of business but for Forest it turned into a disaster and within 18 months Baxter returned to Rangers on a free transfer. After that it was pretty much downhill all the way and after two major operations Jim paid the ultimate price for years of heavy drinking when he died in April 2001. Although he was never the most popular player during his stay on Wearside, he was an exceptional talent and most certainly the finest player I ever played alongside.

The club wasted no time in bringing in a replacement for Baxter's left sided midfield role when a couple of weeks later they signed another Scot who would make a massive impression at the club although this time for all the right reasons! South of the border few people had even heard of Ian Porterfield, yet as soon as he arrived it was apparent to everyone that the club had unearthed a very special talent.

Ironically, like Baxter, Ian had begun his career with Raith Rovers and he was given a real baptism of fire when he made his debut in the Tyne-Wear derby against Newcastle United at Roker Park.

MEETING THE LOCAL YOUNGSTERS JUST BEFORE THE ILL-FATED GAME AGAINST ASHINGTON

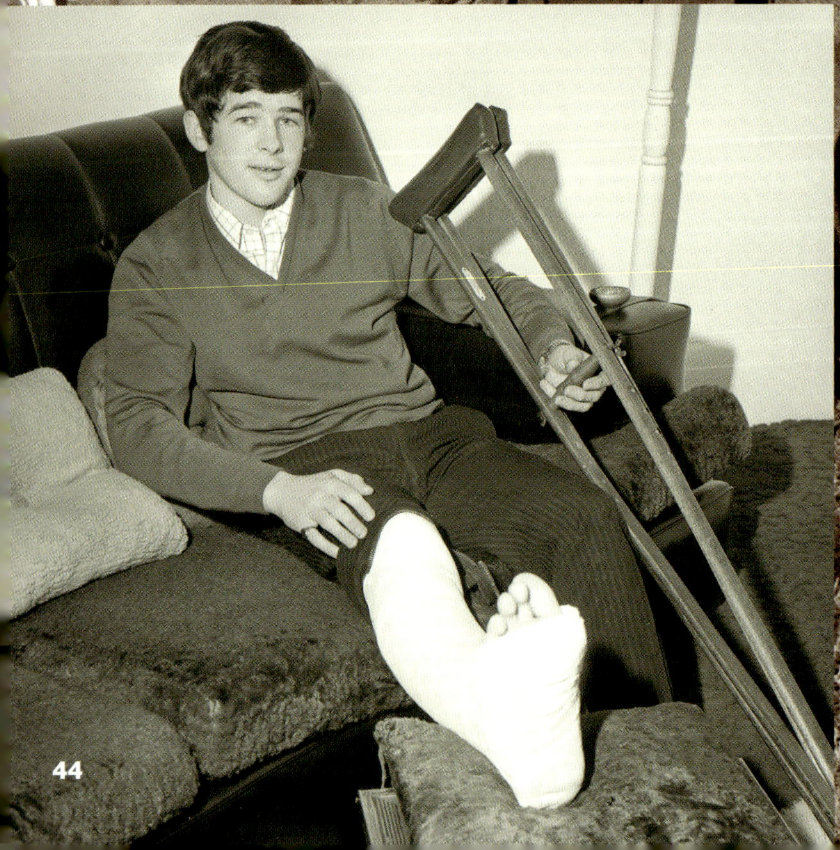

Along with Billy Hughes, Ian became my closest friend during our time together at Sunderland, a lovely guy although not possessing the same wicked sense of humour as Hughesy who was a real wind-up merchant. To give an example, on one occasion I was walking down Fawcett Street in Sunderland town centre with Billy when I spotted this guy coming towards us. 'O God, see this chap,' I said to Billy, 'every time I come into town I bump into him. He seems to know everything about me, the club, my friends, my family but I haven't a clue who he is!' Sure enough, the guy spots me and heads over and as usual starts to rabbit on about this and that when Hughesy interrupts him: 'Excuse my Bobby, but aren't you going to introduce us?' Well, you can imagine how I felt, so I mumbled something about him being a good friend of mine and the guy continues only for Billy to pipe up again: 'Yes, but what's his name?. 'The b******', I thought, 'what the hell can I say now?' Fortunately the guy got me off the hook by introducing himself although to this day I still don't have a clue who he was. But that was typical of Billy, a real joker and a great character to have in the dressing room even if he was bloody annoying at times!

I had hoped to make my return to the first team during the 1967-68 season and was pretty well on course when I headed up to Northumberland for a reserve team game against Northern League side, Ashington. I already had a few reserve team games under my belt and was pretty much back to full fitness but my progress suddenly came to a shuddering halt when I was brought to the ground with a tackle early in the game.

Again I'm pretty certain it was accidental but the result was another broken leg and another couple of months in plaster. It was a heartbreaking moment after such a long haul back and I have to confess that my spirits were pretty low when I was forced to begin the same recovery programme all over again.

The incident at Ashington happened on 2nd January 1968 and a few weeks later it came as no surprise when the news broke that Ian McColl had been relieved of his duties. The team had been struggling near the foot of the table and whilst I always found McColl to be an absolute gentleman, as a manager he had very little and seemed to be totally at a loss as to how to reverse the downward trend. Typically, the speculation regarding the new manager began immediately but few could have predicted that the club would turn to former boss Alan Brown to revive the club's fortunes particularly bearing in mind the nature of his departure almost four years earlier.

The return of 'The Bomber' must have been a huge relief for all of the members of the 1964 promotion squad who still remained at Roker but especially Charlie Hurley who had suffered more than most during the ill-fated McColl era. Brown wasted no time in clearing decks and perhaps made the biggest statement of all just before a pre-season friendly at Middlesbrough which by coincidence happened to be my first appearance in the first team since the two leg breaks.

We were sitting in the dressing room about half an hour before kick-off when Brown walks in ready to deliver his pre-match team talk. 'Right, the first thing is you George,' he said, pointing to our skipper George Kinnell, 'You won't be captain any longer, that role now reverts back to Charlie!' As I would soon discover, that was typical of Alan Brown, no messing around, just straight to the point, job done! It was a great moment for Charlie of course who must have felt elated having been through so much, but I have to say I did feel a certain degree sympathy for George who for all he was Jim Baxter's cousin, wasn't like him at all. George was a decent centre-half, a good old fashioned pro who always gave everything but it was pretty clear that his days with the club were now numbered and sure enough, a few months later he was transferred to Middlesbrough.

Whilst I'd known Alan Brown during his previous reign, that was very much as a junior player where direct contact with him was very limited and it was only now that I was about to find out what it was like to play for a man who had a reputation as one of toughest disciplinarians in football management.

He may well have been a fearsome character but his former players thought the world of him and I think Brian Clough summed up Alan Brown when he said: 'There were times when I detested the man yet moments later he would get me so elated that I would have literally ran through a brick wall for him!'

Apparently while he'd been away Brown had turned to religion and had joined the moral re-armament movement which apparently was based on being pure in body and spirit, so heaven knows what he would have made of my antics at a function in Ryhope only a few weeks earlier! The local football team had made it through to the first round proper of the FA Cup and the Sunderland players had been invited to a special function in the village to celebrate the achievement. I'd been drinking for a few years by then but I'd probably had a bit too much that night which prompted Charlie Hurley to come over and give me a lecture on the evils of drink, particularly for a professional footballer. On and on he went all the time waving a full glass of whisky under my nose until eventually I was forced to race to the toilets where I spent the rest of the night throwing up!

My long awaited return to first team action arrived on 21st September 1968 and ironically, it was against Manchester City again, but this time there was to be no repeat of my debut heroics with the visitors running out comfortable 4-0 winners. Mind you City had an outstanding side at that time which included the likes of Colin Bell, Francis Lee and Mike Summerbee and had lifted the League title the season before. Nevertheless, I suppose the writing was on the wall that afternoon that we faced a tough campaign in the weeks and months that lay ahead.

SHARING A JOKE
WITH 'THE BOMBER'

TRAINING ON ROKER BEACH CIRCA 1968

THERE'S NO PLACE LIKE HOME!

In my view, part of our problem was the lack of an established centre-forward since the departure of Neil Martin who was transferred to Coventry City around about the same time as Alan Brown returned. Whether Brown had anything to do with the move I'm not sure, but Neil was certainly a big miss after he left and I always rated him as one of best strikers around at the time.

The boss tried a number of players in the role and the fact that I actually wore the number nine shirt in five games that season probably tells its own story. In one of those games I was up against Liverpool's legendary centre-half Ron Yeats, a giant man who Bill Shankly described as 'a colossus'. Of course, I didn't have a hope against him physically but Alan Brown's theory was that the Liverpool stopper wouldn't be able to handle a small, tricky opponent. It didn't work though and I spent most of the game taking a right battering with Yeats enjoying himself taking the piss out of me at every opportunity!

Whilst that particular tactic may not have worked Brown was, without doubt one of the most innovative managers of his generation, taking coaching to a whole new level. One particular routine he introduced during his second spell at the club was 'shadow' training. Basically, this consisted of eleven outfield players attacking a goalkeeper at the opposite end of the park, practising moves without the hindrance of opposition players and when he first described what he was after I don't think I was alone in thinking that he was losing the plot! He would orchestrate proceedings from the front row of the directors' box, balling out instructions which echoed around Roker Park's empty terraces.

Those early sessions were certainly confusing and no sooner had we started an attack, Brown would shout: 'Stop!', and then explain where a certain player should be on the park at that point in the move. It was perhaps no coincidence that Brown had served in the police force as his training sessions always had a regimental feel with each player left in no doubt as to what they should doing. Slowly though, things began to take shape and eventually we developed an almost telepathic understanding which we were able to take into our games in the First Division.

Mind you, if anyone failed to follow his instructions during a first team game Brown would spot it immediately. I remember in one particular game just after I'd taken over the captaincy from Martin Harvey, we were a goal down late in the game and had just won a corner. In accordance with our normal game plan our centre half, Ritchie Pitt came up for the kick and when the ball was cleared for a throw-in I told him to stay up the park to help try and snatch an equaliser.

As soon as we came in the dressing room after the game Brown asked: 'And who told Ritchie to stay up the park after that corner was cleared?' 'That was me boss', I replied, 'I thought it might give us a better chance of scoring.' To which he replied sternly: 'Well it won't happen again will it Bobby?'

That's the way it was with Alan Brown, you had to stick to his instructions regardless of whether you thought he was right or wrong and even his captain wasn't allowed to make tactical decisions during the game.

IN ACTION AGAINST THE GREAT BOBBY MOORE DURING OUR HUMILIATING 8-0 DEFEAT AT WEST HAM IN OCTOBER1968

Another thing that Brown insisted on was his players having total respect for the match officials with only the captain allowed to approach the referee. Mind you, the officials were totally different in those days and most enjoyed an excellent rapport with the players. Perhaps more importantly, the seemed to have a better understanding of the game and were certainly more tolerant when it came to bad language. In particular I remember one referee, a guy called Gordon Hill, who was quite happy to turn a blind eye when you told him he was 'f****** useless'. By the same token, if you made a mistake he would often run past you and comment: 'You think I'm useless? That was f****** rubbish!'

One player who did fall foul of Alan Brown was Ian Porterfield, who was frozen out of the first team for a whole season after questioning the boss' tactics. The incident which sparked the disagreement happened during a close-season tour of Germany in 1969 when the boss decided to play Ian out on the left wing, a ridiculous decision considering his lack of pace. During the first game Ian began drifting inside in search of the ball only for Brown to shout from the touchline: 'Get back out on the wing Porterfield!'

Throughout the tour Brown persisted with the tactics before matters finally came to a head in the dressing room after a game against Eintracht Brunswick when he asked the players if anyone had anything to say. To be honest everyone was fed up with the tactics but it was Ian who spoke up and it developed into a right slanging match. At the time Ian was one of our key players in the squad and pretty much a fixture in the first team but when the team sheet went up for our first home game of the season against Coventry City his name was missing. After that he spent the rest of the season in the reserves and wasn't even allowed to train with the first team squad - he'd crossed 'The Bomber' and he'd paid the ultimate price. Ian was distraught and told me that at one point he'd considered quitting the game and heading back to Scotland before Brown eventually called him in to make peace.

Ian was out for the whole of the 1969-70 season, a campaign that soon developed into a desperate bid for First Division survival. Our performances had been hampered to some degree by injuries to one or two of our key players and Alan Brown decided that perhaps our boots were to blame. At the time most of the lads were wearing the new style boots with a moulded multi-stud sole and one morning the boss came into the dressing room with a job lot of the old traditional boots which he'd purchased from Timpsons shoe shop in town. There must have been thirty or forty pairs of varying sizes and he threw them onto the dressing room floor saying: 'Right, from now on we're wearing these!' The boots were pretty much the same style that my brother George had sent me from Barnsley although perhaps not quite as high around the ankles and the guy in Timpsons must have been over the moon at getting rid of all his old stock! In fairness, one or two of the senior pros still preferred the old traditional leather studs although this was partly because they could cut away some of the leather to reveal the nail heads and therefore give their tackles some extra bite!

HAPPIER TIMES - AT HOME WITH CATHY AND OUR DOG SOPHIE

GORDON HILL. A REFEREE WHO ALWAYS SPOKE HIS MIND

Brown attempted to address our goalscoring problems by bringing in Joe Baker from Nottingham Forest, a former England international centre-forward with a terrific pedigree having previously played for Arsenal and Torino in Italy. The transfer had been funded by the sale of Colin Suggett to West Bromwich Albion during the close season for a fee of £100,000, a record for a North East club at the time.

Speaking personally, I was sorry to see Colin leave because he was an exceptional talent with a eye for goal and was just coming to the peak of his game. He and Colin Todd were local lads who had been chased by numerous clubs before Sunderland finally clinched their signatures and it was disappointing that the club had chosen to cash in one of their prized assets.

In July 1969 Cathy and I were married and immediately moved into a smart club-house in Bywell Avenue and as far as my personal life was concerned I'd never been happier, but on the football front things were far from satisfactory. Alan Brown had angered many supporters when he referred to Sunderland as 'a fringe club' in a newspaper interview and he felt their fury even more so when we were relegated at the end of the 1969-70 season. Many fans had never forgiven Brown for taking the club into the Second Division for the first time in its history in 1958 and the fact that he'd done it again simply diminished his popularity even further.

Nevertheless, he carried on undeterred stating that relegation was little more than an unfortunate blip in his long-term strategy for the club. Brave words, although in fairness the club did have a crop of talented youngsters coming through the ranks and Brown had also been a driving force behind a new training complex in Washington. The boss put his heart and soul into that place and unfortunately he made sure the players did their bit too!

Every day after training he'd have us working up there mixing concrete and laying paths and such like so much so that one or two of us even ended up with cement burns! Brown always mucked in though no matter how menial the task and on numerous occasions he'd have us help him go around the perimeter of the training pitches pulling out these huge nettles. We always wore protective gloves but not Brownie, he would take delight in pulling them out with his bare hands!

Early in our first season in Division Two the club made two significant signings when they landed Dick Malone from Ayr United and Dave Watson who cost a club record of £100,000 when was signed from Rotherham. Again the transfers we funded by the sale of one of our prized assets, this time Colin Todd who joined the Brian Clough revolution at Derby County. Colin was a fabulous player and no stranger to Cloughie who had helped coach him during his youth team days at Roker Park.

A TOUCH OF 'FOOTY-TENNIS' WITH IAN PORTERFIELD AT THE NORTHUMBRIA CENTRE CIRCA 1971

Dave Watson of course would go on to develop into on of the finest central defenders in the English game but Alan Brown saw him very much as a striker and immediately installed him in the number nine shirt. Our trainer Bill Elliott had tracked Dave for months before we actually signed him, watching every Rotherham game where Dave had excelled in the centre of their defence. On numerous occasions he tried to persuade Alan Brown to move Dave back into our defence but the boss was having none of it and it would be another two years before Billy would finally get his way.

We soon discovered that Dave was something of a model professional but on one occasion early in his Roker Park career even he fell foul of Alan Brown's strict disciplinary code. We were heading out to Italy to play in the Anglo Italian Tournament and had been ordered by Brown to meet at Roker Park at 10.30am with our coach departing for Newcastle Airport thirty minutes later. Everyone had arrived except Dave but when eleven o'clock arrived the boss ordered our driver Bob to close the doors and set off for the airport.

We'd only been on the road about fifteen minutes when the lads spotted Dave Watson's father's car chasing after us furiously flashing his lights and blasting his horn. I rushed down to the front of the bus to where Brown was sitting and said: "Excuse me boss, but Dave Watson's just behind us in his dad's car - can we pull over?" At that point our driver instinctively began to slow down only for Brown to snap: "What the hell are you doing Bob? Drive on - he knows where the airport is!"

Fortunately, Dave eventually managed to meet up with us at the airport but he was forced to face the wrath of 'The Bomber' in front of the entire squad. In many ways that incident typified Alan Brown's approach to football management - if there was a matter of principle involved, he always stuck to his guns and there's no question he would have left Dave behind just to make his point even though he was one of our best players.

In our first season back in Division Two we finished in a comfortable mid-table position although there was little I can remember about that particular season other than smashing a goalpost in an away fixture at Swindon. It was a bizarre incident which happened when I raced after a ball that was going out of play just past the Swindon goal and I grabbed the post to avoid crashing into the advertising hoarding behind the goal.

Unfortunately, the post was rotten at the bottom and even my light weight was sufficient to bring the whole structure crashing to the ground and the game was held up for the best part of half an hour while the Swindon ground staff carried out the necessary repairs!

ONE OF ALAN BROWN'S MORE UNUSUAL TRAINING ROUTINES

29TH NOVEMBER 1972, THE TURNING POINT IN OUR FORTUNES
BOB STOKOE IS APPOINTED SUNDERLAND MANAGER

The following season saw a vast improvement in our fortunes when we finished in fifth place. As the 1972-73 season approached there was an air of optimism around Roker Park and few could have predicted the disappointing start to the campaign that would unfold culminating in a disastrous 5-1 defeat at Oxford. I was on target that day but that gave me little comfort as we headed back to Wearside with our promotion hopes seemingly in tatters. One point from our next three games had the vultures gathering and I suppose it came as no surprise when it was announced that Alan Brown had been sacked. The players, almost to a man were absolutely devastated having developed such a close bond with the man.

In many ways Alan Brown was ahead of his time and he was certainly a leading innovator when it came to coaching and tactics. Perhaps it's no surprise that so many of his players went on to become successful managers or coaches in their own right none more so than Brian Clough who often paid tribute to his former boss. Of course former Sunderland boss Martin O'Neill will owe much of his managerial success to the years he played under Clough at Nottingham Forest so perhaps Alan Brown's legacy still lives on at Sunderland Football Club after all!

Billy Elliott was given the role of caretaker-manager whilst the club set about finding Alan Brown's replacement and in only his second game in charge at Carlisle he took the decision to move Dave Watson back to the centre of our defence. To be honest Dave didn't play too well that afternoon and was probably to blame for two of their goals in the 4-3 defeat and anyone watching him that day would certainly have been hard pressed to imagine that he would go on to win 65 caps for England.

A few weeks after Brown's departure the club announced that they had appointed former Blackpool boss Bob Stokoe as our new manager although to be honest the news wasn't greeted with universal enthusiasm by our fans given his strong Newcastle United connections. Stokoe had played the best part of his playing career at St James' Park but his managerial credentials were impressive and he had hit the headlines the year before when he led Blackpool to an unlikely victory in the Anglo-Italian Cup.

A few days after Bob was appointed I asked him for a meeting to clarify my position as team captain. I came straight to the point and told him that whilst I would be delighted to continue, if he wanted to make a change there would be no problem as far as I was concerned. He seemed to appreciate gesture and told me that he would just leave things as they were for the time being and we'd see how things developed. Thank goodness he took that decision otherwise I might not have been given the opportunity to fulfil a boyhood dream and lift the FA Cup at Wembley as few months later!

DAVE WATSON PICTURED DURING HIS ROTHERHAM UNITED DAYS

Soon after his arrival at Roker, Bob made a significant appointment when he brought in Arthur Cox as his number two although at the time few people had heard of him. As characters they were totally different with Bob, who was terrible loser, often exploding in the dressing room if things hadn't gone to plan only for the quietly spoken Arthur to come in and calm the waters afterwards. I suppose it was a 'good cop, bad cop' routine but it worked tremendously well. Arthur was an excellent coach and it came as no surprise when he ultimately went on to enjoy a highly successful career in football management in his own right.

One of Stokoe's first decisions at Roker Park was to change our white shorts back to the club's traditional black which certainly won favour with many of our supporters. Alan Brown had introduced the white shorts back in the early '60s apparently to give the team a modern, stylish look but the fans had never been comfortable with the new-look kit.

Bob's reign as Sunderland boss didn't get off to the best of starts when we suffered a 1-0 home defeat at the hands of Burnley but a week later I managed to net the winner when we came from behind to beat Portsmouth 3-2 at Fratton Park. That game was the turning point in our fortunes and by the time the third round of the FA Cup came around a few weeks later confidence was high as we headed down to Nottingham to face Notts County. Speaking personally, I was on something of a high at the time following the birth of our daughter Victoria a few weeks earlier. Cathy and I were delighted of course and I can honestly say I never experienced a greater feeling than when I became a father for the first time.

Anyone who witnessed the game at Meadow Lane would have been hard pushed to imagine that a few months later we'd be the toast of the nation at Wembley as the home side totally dominated the game from the off. Les Bradd had given them a first-half lead and when the same player powered a header goalwards midway through the second period, our cup hopes seemed to be over. It looked a certain goal, but somehow Jim Montgomery got across and produced a truly brilliant save to deny the County striker. It was Monty at his very best and the County players could only hang their heads in disbelief although it came as no surprise to me personally because I'd seen him deny the opposition on so many occasions previously. That save kept us in the game and in the closing stages Dave Watson headed home the equaliser to earn us a replay. It was a great effort by Dave, a thumping header that flew into the net, but had it not been for Monty we would have almost certainly fallen at the first hurdle.

Monty was a brilliant 'keeper and it always amazed me why he never received full international recognition. Apart from Gordon Banks, I reckon there wasn't a better goalkeeper in the English game and in my view, he should have gone to Mexico with England's 1970 World Cup Squad.

Echo

SUNDERLAND

SPORT
EDITIO

SATURDAY, JANUARY 13, 1973

goal
oker
Cup

rland - - - - 1

of a physical battle
round F.A. Cup-tie at
lucky to be only one
hich saw Bradd (29
r-cut chances shaped

esolute County defence could
efensive conflict to throw a
usly determined to correct

RGUS

ome-back, having

JOHN LATHAN

RICHIE PITT

KEITH COL

FIVE FOR SALE

MANAGER Bob Stokoe today announced that Sunderland have decided on a mid-season pruning of their staff and named five young players, all with first team experience, who are now available for transfer.

They are Derek Forster, Richie Pitt, Brian Chambers, Keith Coleman, and John Lathan.

All are youth team products and three of them — Forster, Pitt, and Lathan — have played First Division football.

Mr Stokoe said: "We are circularizing clubs advising them that we will consider offers. We are not naming any figure and if after a time there have been no reasonable offers we will consider letting them go on loan to any club which needs help.

"These are all you

The fact that Alex Stepney of Manchester United was picked ahead of him spoke volumes for the selection process in those days when North-East based players rarely got a look-in.

After the Notts County game the Footy Echo carried the headline: 'Watson goal keeps Roker men in Cup', but also on the front page was the news that Stokoe had put no fewer than five players on the transfer list, John Lathan, Ritchie Pitt, Keith Coleman, Derek Forster and Brian Chambers. The decision to put Ritchie on the list surprised me most of all because he'd already had considerable experience in the top division and the fact that he was immediately approached by Arsenal simply illustrates how highly he was rated by others in the game.

Bob's appointment had done little to rekindle the interest of our supporters and attendances remained at an all-time low with only 12,500 turning up to watch us record an emphatic 4-0 victory over Brighton in our previous home game. Amazingly however, over 30,000 were packed onto the Roker terraces for the replay with Notts County, almost as if the missing fans had sensed something special was in the air. In those days the FA Cup was always a massive draw, much more so than it is these days and in many ways it was regarded as a more glamorous competition to win than the League Championship. Nevertheless, that fact alone could hardly explain the sudden upsurge in interest among our fans. The game itself turned out to be a dour encounter and after Dave Watson had given us a second half lead, we were forced into some desperate defending before Dennis Tueart made the game safe when he netted our second in the closing minutes.

Whilst we'd made it through to the next round, our performances in those two games had been less than convincing which probably prompted Bob Stokoe to step into the transfer market to strengthen the squad. His first port of call was St James' Park where he recruited no fewer than three players from his former club. The first to arrive were Ron Guthrie and David Young and they were followed soon afterwards by another defender, Ray Ellison.

Another player to arrive was Billy Hughes' brother John who had made his reputation north of the border with Celtic where he was part of the squad that lifted the European Cup in 1967. He was nicknamed 'Yogi' by the Celtic fans, because of his size and marauding style down the left wing and the chant 'feed the bear!' would often ring around the Parkhead terraces! I remember watching him when Celtic came down to play Sunderland in a pre-season friendly at Roker Park in 1965, it was Jim Baxter's first game for the club but Celtic destroyed them that afternoon winning 5-0 with Hughes running riot down the left flank for most of the game.

BOB STOKOE WITH NEW SIGNINGS RON GUTHRIE & DAVID YOUNG

JOHN HUGHES IN EUROPEAN CUP ACTION AGAINST LEEDS UNITED

READING BOSS CHARLIE HURLEY SIGNING AUTOGRAPHS BEFORE HIS TEAM'S FA CUP FOURTH ROUND TIE AT ROKER PARK.

Whilst John had played his entire career with Celtic as a traditional left-winger, his physical presence had allowed him to develop into a decent striker after he moved south to join Crystal Palace and Bob obviously saw him as an ideal player to wear the number nine shirt at Roker. John made his debut in a home game against Millwall but his Sunderland career turned out to be short-lived when early in the game he sustained an injury that would effectively end his playing days. It was a disaster for the big man who I'm certain would have turned out to be great addition to the squad.

The FA Cup has a reputation of throwing up romantic ties and that was very much the case when the fourth round draw paired us with Fourth Division Reading who were managed by none other than our old team-mate Charlie Hurley. Predictably the tie at Roker created great interest on Wearside and before the game 'The King' received a tremendous reception when he walked out onto the pitch.

Leading up to the game Charlie had predicted a possible upset and that certainly looked to be on the cards when Les Chappell headed his team into the lead midway through the first half. Dennis Tueart grabbed an equaliser before the break and after that we totally dominated the game but couldn't find a way past their goalkeeper Steve Death who was in truly inspirational form.

Finally, in the closing seconds John Lathan broke through to score only to see his effort ruled out for offside. It had been one of those afternoons where nothing had gone for us in front of goal and now we faced a really tricky replay at Elm Park a few days later.

The media had predicted a tough night for us at Reading's tight little ground but early goals from Dave Watson and Dennis Tueart settled the nerves and after I'd netted a third just before the break we were never in any real danger. Reading pulled one back after the break but it was little more than a consolation as we ran out comfortable 3-1 winners. It was a particularly pleasing night for Ritchie Pitt who'd been brought back into the side after David Young had been ruled out through injury. Although Ritchie wouldn't have realised it at the time, he would remain in the side for the rest of the season.

My most vivid memory of that night at Reading was when we were getting changed in the dressing room after the game and suddenly hearing the Sunderland fans singing outside the players' entrance. It was only when we opened the dressing room door and started to make our way out of the ground that we realised that it wasn't our victory they were celebrating, the man they were chanting for was Charlie Hurley.

That illustrates the sort of impression Charlie had made on the fans during his time at Sunderland and in typical fashion he soon appeared to the biggest cheer of the night!

READING 'KEEPER STEVE DEATH WAS IN BRILLIANT FORM THROUGHOUT THE ROKER PARK TIE AND SECURED HIS TEAM A WELL-EARNED REPLAY - HERE HE IS SAVING FROM BILLY HUGHES

KEEPING IN STEP WITH RITCHIE PITT AND VIC HALOM

The fifth round draw the previous Monday lunchtime had handed us a mountainous task when we were drawn away to Liverpool or Manchester City and as we boarded the team coach after the game at Elm Park the news filtered through that City had beaten Liverpool 2-0 in the replay at Maine Road. Not surprisingly, the bookies immediately installed City as favourites to lift the trophy which was fine with us and we were able to approach the game with nothing to lose.

For the game at Reading, Dave Watson had reverted to his old centre-forward role but having lost John Hughes to injury, Bob Stokoe wasted no time in bringing in another centre-forward when he signed Vic Halom from Luton Town. Vic was well known to Bob having played for him when he was manager at Charlton and he was to prove a tremendous signing for us, a traditional style centre-forward with no small degree of skill and a player who could hold the ball up as well as weighing in with his fair share of goals.

The tie at Maine Road brought thousands flocking down from the North East and when we ran out onto the park there was an incredible atmosphere inside the ground with our supporters more than holding their own against the home fans. Everyone outside Sunderland had predicted a comfortable win for City and the opening stages certainly seemed to support the pundits view that City were on course to lift the trophy. Almost from the start the battered our goal and when Tony Towers drove home their opening goal from the edge of the box after only 16 minutes, it looked as though the predicted hiding could be on the cards. Nevertheless, we managed to weather the storm, largely through some excellent defending by the lads at the back, although as half-time approached we had presented little threat to the City goal when a mistake by the 'keeper, Joe Corrigan allowed us back into the game. It was something of a bizarre goal really with City having won a free-kick on the edge of their six-yard box and when Corrigan took the kick before the whistle had blown, referee Ray Tinkler ordered him re-take it. Joe had played the first kick short to Willie Donachie on the edge of the box and he did exactly the same on the re-take only to find that Mickey had been deliberately hiding behind Donachie and was able to nip in, win possession, lob the ball over the City defender's head before running on to drive the ball past the stunned Corrigan and into the net. It was a marvellous piece of ingenuity by Mickey and it got back us into the match which for long periods in that first half had looked beyond us.

The second half began with City in the ascendancy but after 68 minutes we broke away to grab the lead with a brilliantly taken solo goal from Billy Hughes. If Billy had one thing it was pace and after Dennis Tueart released him from the half-way line he raced into the City box and turned inside Jeffries before unleashing a terrific shot high into the net. It was a wonderful effort by Billy and our supporters predictably, were going absolutely crazy.

DAVE WATSON HEADS CLEAR DURING THE FA CUP FIFTH ROUND AGAINST MANCHESTER CITY AT MAINE ROAD

Unfortunately, the lead lasted little more than four minutes when an uncharacteristic error from Monty allowed the home side to grab an equaliser. The goal came when City won a corner on the left and when Summerbee floated the ball over, Jim was under pressure from Rodney Marsh and was unable to prevent the ball sneaking in at the near post. After that it was all City, with Monty more than making up for his error with a string of fine saves to deny the City forwards.

Then with seven minutes to go, Towers body-checked Mickey Horswill and suddenly the two of them were at each others throats. When order was restored Towers was given his marching orders much to the annoyance of the home supporters with Mickey receiving a booking for his part in the incident. Soon afterwards the final whistle blew to end a truly memorable game and to set up a replay that would eventually be voted Roker Park's greatest ever game.

The City players wasted no time in beginning the 'mind games' to try and unsettle our preparations for the game at Roker with Francis Lee announcing to the press: 'I'll forfeit a weeks wages if we don't manage to beat Sunderland in the replay.' Brave words, but he clearly hadn't reckoned with the team spirit and self-belief that Bob Stokoe had instilled in our camp and perhaps more importantly the atmosphere that they would have to face inside Roker Park which was about to be filled to its 52,000 capacity.

To be honest, the City replay was pretty much a complete blur for me personally and the game seemed to go over so quickly that I can remember very few of the details other than the goals. Of course, I'll never forget the incredible atmosphere and I've never heard anything like the noise our fans generated that night, particularly when we opened the scoring with a truly magnificent goal from Vic Halom. The move began out on the left with the ball ending up with me out on the right wing. I pushed the ball on to Vic who was just outside the corner of the penalty area and he unleashed a shot of such power that Joe Corrigan in the City goal could only stand and watch as it flew into the top corner of the net, clipping the inside of the post on the way.

VIC HALOM OPENS THE SCORING - ONE OF ROKER PARK'S GREATEST-EVER GOALS!

BILLY HUGHES FIRES HOME OUR SECOND GOAL IN THE EPIC FIFTH ROUND REPLAY AGAINST MANCHESTER CITY AT ROKER PARK

Then, midway through the first half Roker Park was really rocking when Billy Hughes added a second. I remember taking a long throw-in out on the right which found Billy inside the box and when his first shot was blocked he regained possession, rounded Donachie and drove home a terrific strike.

When we walked off at half-time we could see that the City players were stunned but we knew the game wasn't over by any means and when Francis Lee pulled a goal early in the second half we suddenly had a fight on our hands. We needed some desperate defending as City pressed forward but the lads at the back performed heroically and with just 12 minutes remaining we broke away to score the goal that sealed the match. It actually came when we won possession from a City corner to send Dennis Tueart racing down the right wing and into the box to fire in a shot which Corrigan could only parry and as the ball rolled agonisingly across the face of the goal Hughesy arrived at the far post to fire the ball into the empty net. We knew then the game was over and when the final whistle blew the roar nearly lifted the roof off!

Back in the dressing room everyone wanted to come in to congratulate us and I remember our chairman Keith Collings going around the room shaking the players' hands and just saying: 'Marvellous, bloody marvellous!' Some of the lads were in tears and Ritchie in particular was very emotional, although he told me afterwards that it was more with relief having proved to himself that he could hold his own against some of the best players in the game after Bob Stokoe had cast doubts over his ability.

In the players' lounge afterwards the City players were having a bit of a go at Joe Corrigan particularly about the first goal when the City 'keeper had stood motionless as Vic's shot flew into the net. 'What happened on that first goal Joe?' asked Francis Lee, 'You didn't move a muscle!' 'Well I thought it was going wide.' replied Joe. 'Going wide?', said Lee, 'It was going wide alright wasn't it, you big useless bugger!' In all fairness, I don't think there was a goalkeeper anywhere in the world who could have stopped that shot but that didn't stop the City players winding up poor Joe!

The following morning the whole town was buzzing and with the draw handing us a home tie against Second Division Luton Town, the semi-finals were now in sight. Everyone was talking about the City game the night before and I remember standing outside the main entrance at Roker Park chatting to the journalist Arthur Appleton when a woman came up to me and said: 'You're Bobby Kerr aren't you? I listened to the game on the radio last night and I cried at the end - it was so wonderful!' It was amazing, the game had captivated the thoughts of just about everyone in the town and even people who didn't have the slightest interest in the game were now being swept away by the emotion of it all.

DRESSING ROOM CELEBRATIONS AFTER OUR UNFORGETTABLE VICTORY OVER MANCHESTER CITY

RON GUTHRIE SWIVELS TO VOLLEY HOME OUR SECOND GOAL IN THE SIXTH ROUND VICTORY OVER LUTON TOWN AT ROKER PARK

In all fairness, it had been a truly incredible night and in all my years at the club I'd never experienced noise like it. Legend has it that the morning after the game one of the groundsmen was going about his duties at Roker Park when he noticed a lone figure wandering around the Fulwell End terracing and staring up at the roof.

When the groundsman approached him, the guy explained that he was a London-based journalist who had been reporting on the game the night before.

'In all my years of watching football I've never heard noise like that. It's a wonderful gimmick, but where are the hidden amplifiers?' he asked. 'Amplifiers?' replied the groundsman, 'There's no bloody amplifiers here mate. What you heard last night was the Roker Roar!'

After our performance against City everyone seemed to be confident we would beat Luton comfortably at Roker but Bob Stokoe was having none of it and during the week leading up to the game he hammered home the point citing the fact that up until then they hadn't conceded a goal in the competition. John Aston was singled out as their danger man and the former Manchester United winger was in fine form having scored both the goals that had knocked Newcastle United out of the competition in the fourth round.

The game itself turned into something of an anti-climax and whilst we struggled to produce a serious threat on the Luton goal in the first period, Dick Malone had done an excellent job in nullifying the threat of John Aston. The vital breakthrough came ten minutes into the second half when Dave Watson came up for a corner to power home a header and after that we were pretty much in control of the game which was made safe when Ron Guthrie popped up with a rare goal when he swivelled to volley home the second. It had been an efficient rather than an inspired performance but we were into the semi-finals and all thoughts were now focussed on the draw the following Monday.

In those days before Sky TV and such like, the draw was always broadcast over the radio on a Monday lunchtime and I think the whole of Wearside must have had their ears glued to the radio to find out who we would be playing. Bob Stokoe had assembled the lads at the Roker Hotel and there was huge cheer when the draw paired us with Arsenal or Chelsea who were due to replay their tie later in the week. A 2-1 victory for Arsenal meant we would be meeting Bertie Mee's side at Hillsborough, some challenge considering that only two years before they had become only the second team in the twentieth century to win the league and cup double!

ON CUE WITH MONTY AND BILLY HUGHES

LEADING OUT 'THE LADS' FOR THE SEMI-FINAL AGAINST ARSENAL AT HILLSBOROUGH

Cup fever was now sweeping across Wearside with everyone desperate to see the big game and I soon lost count of the number of times I was approached for tickets. Since the City game the club had been issuing different coloured vouchers at home league games and if your particular colour was drawn, then you were lucky enough to be able to purchase a ticket for the semi-final.

In fairness to the club I suppose it was the fairest way to deal with such a massive demand for tickets but I couldn't help thinking about the hard-core fans who used to turn up week after week when our attendances often struggled to top 12,000. Tragically, some of those supporters seemed certain to miss out on one of the club's biggest games for years.

Our improved form had seen us surge up the league and whilst Bob Stokoe had brought in one or two new faces, the squad was largely the one that Alan Brown had left behind and people often ask me to explain exactly what Bob did to turn things around. To be honest, there wasn't anything specific but his approach to football management was much more easy-going than Brown's, who ran the club with rigid discipline from top to bottom.

Stokoe, on the other hand, allowed the flair players to go out and express themselves and often his pre-match instructions consisted of little more than: 'I know how good you are, now go out there and do what you do in training and enjoy yourselves!' That's not to say he was an easy touch and if you stepped out of line he could be just as hard as Brown if he felt the need. In short though, he simply gave us that bit of freedom on the park and it worked.

Cup fever was now sweeping across Wearside prompting Bob Stokoe to take us away to relax and we spent the week leading up to the semi in the quiet and comfortable surroundings of the Palace Hotel in Buxton. Arsenal were only a point behind league-leaders Liverpool and were in with a chance of pulling off the double again with Alan Ball stating in one interview: 'It's impossible for us to lose, we're a much better team than Sunderland and far too experienced!' I remember the lads having a good laugh when we read that - Francis Lee had said something similar before the City replay and look what happened to them!

In football, there are games when one particular player hits a purple patch and in the first half of the semi-final at Hillsborough that certainly applied to Vic Halom who simply ran the Arsenal defence ragged. On his game there were few better front men than Vic and that afternoon he gave the Gunners centre-half Jeff Blockley a torrid time with his robust, strong-running play.

ENJOYING A ROUND OF GOLF AT BUXTON WITH MONTY, JOE BOLTON AND RITCHIE PITT

We began the game attacking the giant Kop End of the ground which was packed with our fans and they roared us on brilliantly right from the off. The noise was incredible and whilst we didn't need much motivation that day, that just gave us the extra lift and confidence to take the game to Arsenal.

Vic was like a man possessed and when Mickey Horswill lofted a high ball through the middle he raced into the box while Blockley hesitated and rounded Bob Wilson to slot the ball into the empty net. Poor Blockley was having a nightmare and Vic could easily have had a hat-trick before the break only to be denied by a couple of smart saves by the Arsenal 'keeper. Mind you, we needed Monty to pull off a miraculous save just before the interval when George Armstrong's shot was deflected and looked certain to be heading into the corner of the net.

BATTLING FOR POSSESSION WITH ARSENAL'S ALAN BALL DURING THE SEMI-FINAL AT HILLSBOROUGH

Amazingly, there was an air of disappointment in our dressing room at half-time and the general feeling was that with a bit of luck, we could have been two or three goals in front. A single goal was a slender lead particularly against a team like Arsenal who had come back to overturn a two goal deficit in the semi-final against Stoke City the year before and whilst Bob Stokoe told us to keep it tight at the back he stressed the importance of trying to grab a second goal.

The second period continued in pretty much the same vein with Arsenal unable to make any headway against our defence which to a man was performing brilliantly. Ten minutes into the half Bertie Mee had brought on John Radford in an attempt to improve their attacking options but there was little threat and on sixty-four minutes came the goal that brought our Wembley dream a step closer. It began when I took a throw-in out on the right which found Dennis Tueart on the corner of the box and when he headed on it, Bob Wilson began to advance. The ball didn't carry though and when Billy Hughes back -headed it on again, it caught the Arsenal 'keeper off his line and the ball looped over him and into the far corner of the net.

Arsenal to a man looked stunned but predictably they rallied as the game headed towards the closing stages and when Charlie George netted with only six minutes remaining their mood changed dramatically. It was a blow and Monty had come so close to saving George's close-range effort, getting a full hand on the shot only to see the ball squirm from his reach and creep over the line. After that it was 'backs to the wall' stuff with the game reaching fever pitch as we entered the final minutes then, with only seconds remaining Arsenal won a corner on the right. The tension was unbearable as we braced ourselves for the Gunners last assault on our goal but as Armstrong and Radford deliberated over who would take the kick, referee David Smith blew the final whistle!

We had made it to Wembley and the scenes that followed will live with me forever with many of our players in tears and our massed ranks of supporters celebrating in the grandest fashion imaginable. When we eventually made it back to the dressing room we could hear them chanting for Bob Stokoe, the man they now referred to as 'The Messiah' and he duly obliged by walking out to applaud them. I'd never known Bob to be emotional but that afternoon he was in tears as he stood with his arms raised to salute the fans before declaring to the surrounding press and media: 'There'll never be another moment like this!'.

Suddenly, Sunderland was the talk of the whole nation and it seemed you couldn't switch on the television or radio without our FA Cup exploits being the main topic of discussion.

DEFENSIVE WALL - PROTECTING THE PARTS THE BALL MIGHT REACH!

EMOTIONAL AT THE FINAL WHISTLE, 'THERE'LL NEVER BE ANOTHER MOMENT LIKE THIS!' BOB SAID AFTERWARDS

MEETING ROD STEWART AND THE FACES AT THE MECCA BALLROOM IN SUNDERLAND SHORTLY BEFORE THE 1973 FA CUP FINAL

Our opponents in the final were to be none other than arch-rivals Leeds United who had beaten Wolves with a solitary Billy Bremner goal in the other semi-final at Maine Road. If the Manchester City and Arsenal games had provided a severe test of our abilities, then Don Revie's team most certainly represented the ultimate challenge.

Apart from challenging for another league title, Leeds were FA Cup holders and had also reached the final of the European Cup-Winners Cup where they were to meet AC Milan a few days after the Wembley final. Although, their team included many top-class players, their intimidating style had made them one of the most hated teams in the country with just about every neutral fan willing us to beat them in the final.

There was certainly no love lost between our managers who as players had also been in opposition in the 1955 FA Cup final when Bob's Newcastle United side triumphed over Revie's Manchester City. Bob's dislike of Revie was well known to us although speaking personally I had no idea why he held the Leeds boss in such contempt. It was only a few years later when the Daily Mirror ran a feature called 'The Revie File' that allegations of match fixing began to emerge.

One of those games was back in Leeds United's Second Division days when Revie allegedly approached Bob, who was manager of Bury at the time, and offered him money in return for making sure his team lost the game. Bob not surprisingly, had reacted angrily and was so disgusted that he hadn't spoken to Revie since. If nothing else Bob was as honest as they come and above all, he was a winner who loved to come out on top even in the most meaningless five-a-side game. Revie can't have known him that well because the idea of Bob being persuaded to throw a match really was unthinkable.

The week after the semi-final we headed across to Lancashire to record 'Sunderland All The Way', a commercial venture that had been set up by a guy who was supposed to be an official club agent although, to the best of my knowledge we never made a penny out of the venture.

Local comedian Bobby Knoxall, one of the funniest men I've ever met, joined us at the Strawberry Studios in Stockport where the recording went brilliantly and to be honest all the lads had a great laugh even though the promised riches never actually materialised at the end of the day!

A few days later, we met Rod Stewart and The Faces who were appearing at the Mecca Ballroom at the time and the lads had a tremendous time chatting to Rod who was and still is a great football fan.

MEETING THE LEGENDARY RAICH CARTER AND HIS SON RAICH JUNIOR

TRAINING AT SELSDON PARK

Another legendary figure I met around this time was Raich Carter who had captained the Sunderland team when they had last won the FA Cup in 1937. I spent a good few hours chatting to him as well as having a bit of a kick about with him and his son Raich Junior for the benefit of the nearby press photographers.

I found Raich to be a fascinating character and it was wonderful to hear how he had joined the club as a youngster and had went on to captain what many regard as Sunderland's greatest ever team. Having been born and bred on Wearside, he remained the only Sunderland captain ever to lift the FA Cup, the club's 3-1 victory over Preston North End in 1937 being their only success in English football's most famous competition. I remember thinking at the time how much of an achievement it would be if I could emulate that feat in the forthcoming final!

Newspaper interviews were coming thick and fast and apart from training, almost every day was taken up with meeting the press and it was during one of these interviews that Bob Stokoe first referred to me as his 'Little General'. Former Sunderland legend Len Shackleton, a good friend of Bob's, was writing for The People newspaper at the time and before he ran the story, he persuaded me to have my photograph taken dressed up in a general's uniform. Once the photo appeared in print the name stuck and to this day loads of people still refer to me as 'The Little General'.

Our exploits in the FA Cup had resulted in something of a fixture pile-up and the four weeks between the semi-final and final we played no fewer than eight league games, the last of these against Orient the Monday before the final. Because the game was in London, Bob Stokoe had decided that we should to stay down to prepare for the final and after a 1-1 draw at Brisbane Road, we headed down to Croydon where we set up base at Selsdon Park Hotel and Golf Club.

Apart from some light training, we spent most of the time relaxing, mainly out on the golf course. Not surprisingly, the media were out in force chasing interviews although they can't have reckoned with Billy Hughes who had managed to acquire a laughing box of all things. Every time they got under way with an interview, Hughesy would set the thing away in the background!

It can't have been much fun for the poor press guys but they took it in good part and as far as the squad was concerned it worked wonders to settle any nerves that might have been surfacing as the big game approached. To be honest, I can't ever remember being so relaxed leading up to an important game and they don't come any bigger than the FA Cup Final.

WITH BOB STOKOE ON THE BANKS OF THE WEAR. SHIPBUILDING WAS A MASSIVE INDUSTRY IN SUNDERLAND AT THE TIME AND THE SHIPYARDS USED TO PROVIDE LARGE NUMBERS OF SUPPORTERS WHO USED TO MAKE THE SHORT JOURNEY TO ROKER PARK WHEN THEIR SATURDAY MORNING SHIFT HAD ENDED

Bob Stokoe was doing his bit by winding up the Leeds United camp, complaining that the Yorkshire club had been given a distinct advantage when their fans had been allocated the terracing adjacent to the Wembley tunnel whereas our fans were at the opposite end of the ground.

Bob argued that as the teams came out onto the pitch it would be the Leeds fans who would be heard first as the teams walked down the tunnel. It was a minor point perhaps, but Bob milked it to the limit just to wind up the Leeds United camp and by all accounts it worked a treat with reports suggesting the mood among Revie's players was far from the carefree atmosphere that we were enjoying at Selsdon Park.

On the Wednesday before the game we travelled up to Wembley and I got my first glimpse of the ground that had hosted so many great games over the years. England, of course, had lifted the World Cup there in 1966 but I couldn't help thinking back how Jim Baxter had sunk the English with two classic performances on the hallowed turf.

To think that I would be leading Sunderland down that famous tunnel sent a shiver down my spine and as we wandered off the pitch I gave one last look up to the Royal Box and tried to imagine what it would be like if I was the one climbing the stairs to lift the famous old trophy a few days later.

The Sportswriters' Dinner in Bloomsbury was our port of call on the Thursday evening and on the eve of the final we got down to the serious business of preparing for the big game. Unlike the Alan Brown era, Bob allowed the squad to have much more of a say when it came to tactics and often the players would decide between themselves who would be marking a particular opposition player. If we were to believe the media, Eddie Gray was our main threat and it was agreed that Dick Malone and I would work together to contain him. By the same token Dave Watson and Ritchie Pitt discussed at length how they would deal with Leeds' strikers Allan Clarke and Mick Jones. Both were excellent front men although Jones was probably stronger in the air so it was decided that Dave would mark Jones leaving Ritchie to pick up Clarke.

The relaxed mood continued on the morning of the game when we occupied ourselves with a game of snooker before boarding the coach around mid-day to make the short journey up to the stadium. I suppose it was only when we arrived on the outskirts of Wembley and spotted the thousands of fans heading towards the ground that the pre-match nerves kicked in. The place was awash with red and white and it seemed that the whole of Wearside had made the journey south.

There was so much activity in our dressing room with well-wishers and such like that the couple of hours leading up to the game passed quickly and in no time at all we were standing alongside the Leeds players in the tunnel. Bob Stokoe and Don Revie were leading the teams out and as we waited for the referee's signal to proceed, I noticed them have a few words with one another which surprised me a little, given the supposed animosity between the pair, although perhaps Bob was just being polite for the sake of the cameras!

F.A. CUP FINAL
1973

ONE OF MY PROUDEST MOMENTS - LINED UP AT WEMBLEY
WAITING TO BE PRESENTED TO THE DUKE OF KENT

CONTESTING POSSESSION WITH NORMAN 'BITES YOUR LEGS' HUNTER

Our general game plan was to take the game to Leeds from the off and try to grab an early goal and when I won the toss I decided to attack the goal behind which our 20,000 or so fans were amassed. I remember thinking that Billy Bremner and I must have been the two smallest captains in FA Cup final history! Heavy rain had fallen leading up to the match which made conditions a little tricky and probably helped Ritchie Pitt avoid a booking in the opening minutes when he brought Allan Clarke to the ground with a shuddering tackle. Soon after, Monty had to push away a cross from Peter Lorimer and then Dave Watson got in a vital block to deny Clarke but after that we more than held our own. The breakthrough we had craved came just after the half hour when I sent in a right-wing cross which I thought I'd over hit but David Harvey in the Leeds goal was forced to tip it over for a corner just as it appeared to be dropping under the bar.

Hughesy took the corner out on the left and when his cross dropped into the box Vic pushed it forward for Ian to cushion the ball on his left thigh before sending a terrific right-foot volley crashing past Harvey and high into the net. Ian wasn't a noted goal scorer and was so left-sided it wasn't true but the shot on his weaker right foot was truly stunning and sent the players and fans absolutely wild with delight. The Leeds players were visibly stunned but we knew we still had a mountain to climb and needed to regain our composure quickly. The game plan had worked a treat particularly as far as Eddie Gray was concerned. Dick and I had him in our pocket from the start and as we trooped off at half-time it was very much a case of so far so good.

As expected, Leeds came at us strongly after the break but we were defending magnificently and actually came close to a second goal through Ron Guthrie of all people whose drive from the edge of the box flew narrowly past the top corner and into the side netting. Soon afterwards came the moment that is certain to be etched in FA Cup final history for all time. Reaney began the move crossing deep from the right to find Cherry racing in at the far post to send in a header that looked a goal all the way. Monty, diving to his left somehow managed to push the ball away but only to Lorimer on the edge of the six-yard box who instinctively drove the ball goalwards.

To be honest, with Monty on the ground I was just waiting for the net to bulge and there was a moment of utter disbelief when he somehow managed to get across and throw out an arm to divert Lorimer's shot onto the bar before Dick Malone hooked it clear.

It was a truly amazing save that literally took your breath away and at that moment you could see the energy draining out of the Leeds players. There was still a quarter of the game remaining but that save seemed to galvanise our belief that this was to be our day.

THE TOSS-UP WITH LEEDS UTD SKIPPER BILLY BREMNER

'PORTERFIELD - ONE-NIL!'

MONTY'S FINEST HOUR

With fifteen minutes to go Leeds brought on Terry Yorath to replace Eddie Gray who for all the pre-match predictions had hardly featured in the game. Whilst Leeds were still enjoying their share of possession, they never really threatened our goal again and Vic Halom could have made the game safe but for a brilliant fingertip save by David Harvey. The final minutes were nerve-wracking of course and must have been unbearable for our supporters in the stadium and the people back home on Wearside, but Wembley can hardly have heard a loader roar than when referee Ken Burns blew the final whistle. It had been a truly unbelievable performance and no one will ever forget the sight of Bob Stokoe racing across the Wembley turf to congratulate Monty. It is an image that will remain one of Wembley's greatest moments and one which is preserved for all time by a wonderful statue outside Sunderland's Stadium of Light.

We were racing around hugging each other and even good old Johnny Watters was out there on the pitch joining in the celebrations. I remember racing to Bob Stokoe and being hoisted in the air by the boss when it suddenly dawned on me that I wasn't wearing my false teeth. A few of the lads wore them and before the game they were all put in boxes alongside our bench on the touchline. Fortunately, I managed to find mine just in time for the presentation otherwise the Duchess of Kent might have received something of a shock seeing my toothless grin!

No words can describe the feeling of lifting the FA Cup to the massed ranks of Sunderland fans; it really was a moment that defies description. I knew then that whatever I might go on to achieve in the game, nothing would be able replace that afternoon at Wembley.

What perhaps a lot of people don't realise is that after holding the cup aloft, I lost my footing as I made my way down the steps from the Royal Box and dropped the bloody thing! Fortunately Monty was just behind me and helped recover the situation and then just to add to the confusion, I suddenly realised that I'd forgot to pick up my winners medal and had to signal to Ritchie Pitt to do the honours for me!

Back down on the pitch referee Ken Burns came over to congratulate me before handing me the match ball. It was a great gesture by Ken and it would have been a priceless memento to add to my collection, but I felt the man who should have the ball was our goal scorer Ian Porterfield and when I handed it to him he was overjoyed. Back in the dressing room it was pandemonium with everyone singing, champagne corks popping and when we finally managed to get into the bath, football writer Bob Cass was promptly launched in fully clothed to join us. Bob thought it was brilliant and was just delighted at being allowed to join in the celebrations. If I remember rightly, he left Wembley Stadium that night wearing one of our tracksuits carrying his wet clothes over his arm!

No words can describe the feeling of lifting the FA Cup to the massed ranks of Sunderland fans; it really was a moment that defies description.

SO
ORWICH
SUP

UMBRO
International

ARTHUR COX AND I PARADE THE CUP IN FRONT OF OUR MAGNIFICENT SUPPORTERS - ARTHUR RARELY SHOWED HIS EMOTIONS BUT ON THIS OCCASION EVEN HE COULDN'T CONTAIN HIS JOY

F.A. CUP FINAL
1973

The more formal celebrations took place at the Park Lane Hotel during which as captain, I was asked to give the customary speech and when I stood and began to speak, Bob Cass shouted out: "Stand up, we can't see you!" This was typical of Bob and I responded immediately by climbing onto my chair to a huge round of applause before proceeding to deliver my speech from my newly elevated position! I then had to race upstairs to do an interview for the BBC who'd set up a studio to go out live on 'Match of the Day' and in my haste I tripped on the top stair ending up going full length on the landing. As I stumbled I'd thrust my arms forward to break my fall when I suddenly heard the seam tear on the back of my jacket. It was pretty much torn along the full length with only the collar holding the thing together and my first thoughts were to get back to my room for a change of clothing. Unfortunately, there was no time as the BBC staff quickly ushered me into the makeshift studio where I was immediately swept in front of the cameras and I ended up going out to a nationwide audience with my jacket literally hanging off my back!

The following morning I was up quite early and after a quick shower I'd just finished getting 'suited and booted' in true Alan Brown fashion when the press appeared at the door wanting a photograph of me with the FA Cup. I duly agreed but they insisted they needed me in bed with the trophy as if I'd just woken up so I had to take off my jacket, shirt and tie and climb into bed wearing my trousers and shoes!

Our fans were no doubt desperate to welcome us back to Wearside but the fixture pile-up meant that we still had two league games to play the first of which was an away game against Cardiff City. I don't know if it's something of a record but we could have well been the only FA Cup winners to leave the country before returning home with the trophy!

Cardiff needed a point to avoid relegation so were well satisfied when the game ended in a 1-1 draw. The following morning we set off on the long journey north although we had no idea of the scale of the welcome that awaited us. Fans sporting banners and flags began appearing when we reached Scotch Corner and when we pulled off the motorway at Durham there was an open-topped bus waiting to take us on the final lap of the journey.

The driver told me that the bus had had its top torn off when its driver had inadvertently driven under a low level bridge some months earlier and the bus company had worked around the clock since the final to get it prepared for our homecoming!

To be honest, the journey back to Roker Park defies description and as soon as we left Durham the road was lined with ecstatic fans, young and old with many weeping tears of joy.

'STAND UP, WE CAN'T SEE YOU!'

THE MORNING AFTER THE NIGHT BEFORE

FAWCETT STREET, 8TH MAY 1973 - WHAT A HOMECOMING!

By the time we reached Herrington, there was just a sea of people with quite a number hanging from trees and even balanced on the rooftops and from then on we were forced to proceed at crawling pace until we eventually reached Fawcett Street which had been specially decorated for the occasion. By now an enormous procession of fans were following us on the last lap of our journey over Wearmouth Bridge, down Roker Avenue and finally to Roker Park where it had all began with that tentative victory over Notts County a few months earlier.

The scenes were just as amazing inside the ground which was packed to the rafters and I remember some supporters had built a mock coffin carrying the inscription: 'Leeds United - Died 1973', which they carried around the ground with a funeral-style procession before placing it on the centre spot! The celebrations went on well into the night before Bob Stokoe finally brought proceedings to a close when he took the microphone and said:

'You have given us a night which we will never, ever forget in a million years. We believe we did something for you on Saturday but you have done something very special for us tonight!'

Bob would be out on the pitch again the following night when the celebrations were meant to continue in our final home game of the season against Queens Park Rangers but this time he would be addressing the fans in totally different circumstances. Before the match there were no problems when I led the team out carrying the FA Cup and when the game kicked off the trophy was placed on a table at the tunnel entrance. Rangers had already clinched promotion so the result was pretty meaningless to both clubs and to be fair the last thing we needed was another competitive game because we were all absolutely shattered after the amazing events of the previous few days. The problems began early in the game when Stan Bowles, Rangers' talented but controversial midfielder decided to attempt to knock the FA Cup from its precarious perch and when he succeeded many of our fans were furious.

That pretty much set the tone for the remainder of the game and after half-time things boiled over when Mickey Horswill was sent off, which prompted a mini pitch invasion by our supporters. With things threatening to turn ugly the referee took the players off the pitch and Bob was forced to go out and plead with the fans to be calm and not spoil what had been one of the greatest weeks in the club's history. After a few minutes delay the game restarted with Rangers, not surprisingly running out 3-0 winners. It was a sad end to a truly incredible few days.

After our cup exploits all the players were in demand and one or two managed to secure sponsorship deals with local car dealers which effectively meant they had the use of a brand new vehicle providing they were happy to drive around with their name on the side advertising the particular dealership.

BOB AND I BEING MOBBED AS WE CARRY THE FA CUP DOWN THE ROKER PARK TUNNEL

Mercedes
Renault
Volkswagen
XGR 888L
CONTACT Head Office
Newcastle Road, Sunderland
for further details Telephone : 58225

Strangely, I hadn't been approached by anyone until one Sunday morning I received a phone call from a guy who introduced himself as Mike Rowlands of the Mill Garages. "Good Morning Bobby, Mike Rowlands here from Mill Garages," he began, "Listen Bobby, we'd like to give you a new car, any chance you could pop down to the showroom in the morning and we'll sort out the details?"

To be honest I didn't know what to make of the call because he went on to insist that they weren't just offering me the use of the car, they were actually going to give it to me, a brand-new Audi at that! I told the guy to ring back in twenty minutes so I could gather my thoughts and I turned to Cathy and said: "I think I've just had a dodgy phone call - there's a guy just been on who says he's going to give us a new Audi!" Sure enough though, twenty minutes later the phone rang and arrangements were made for me to meet him at the Audi Garage in Fulwell the following morning. I was still a little sceptical when I walked into the showroom but sure enough, Mike was there to meet us.

"There they are Bobby," he said pointing to the full range of brand new Audis on display, "Just pick which one you want and it's yours." I still wasn't convinced and asked: "Listen Mike, have I got this right, are you saying you're actually going to give me the car?" "Absolutely, right Bobby," he replied, "All we ask is you bring the FA Cup along and have your photo taken with the car. Now, which one do you want?"

I immediately looked at the array of shining cars and settled on the biggest and the best, a beautiful, gleaming Audi A6 - well, you don't look a gift horse in the mouth!

That Audi car was one of the rare bonuses I received following our cup triumph and whilst each player had received £1,000 from the club after our Wembley victory, I was still on a basic wage of just £65 a week plus £25 appearance money. That wasn't bad compared to the average working wage which I think was around £50 a week at the time but in relation to First Division clubs we were way behind and I knew that many top-flight players were receiving almost double our wages. We were still in the Second Division of course but our performances in the FA Cup had thrown some of our players into the limelight and I suppose most of us felt we deserved something of an increase in way of appreciation. The problem was, the government had just imposed a national pay freeze which meant that employers couldn't give employees a salary increase even if they wanted to although anyone was free to move to another job and negotiate whatever salary they wanted.

That fact alone spelled the end of the cup-winning team as a unit and during the following season, First Division scouts were regular visitors at our games. Our three best players were probably Monty, Dave Watson and Dennis Tueart although Jim was Sunderland through and through having been born just a few miles from Roker Park and there was no way I could see him leaving the club willingly. Dave would soon pick up his first cap for England so it was hard to see the club hanging on to him if the big boys came calling.

THE FA CUP, HELD BY JOE BOLTON, PACKED AND READY TO LEAVE SUNDERLAND ON ITS WAY BACK TO THE FA

SIGHT SEEING IN BUDAPEST ON THE BANKS OF THE DANUBE

OUR FIRST VENTURE INTO EUROPEAN COMPETITION BROUGHT A 2-0 VICTORY OVER VASAS BUDAPEST

Dennis was also being linked with a move to the First Division and his performance in our first venture into Europe against Vasas Budapest certainly did his chances of a move to the top flight no harm at all. Our 2-0 victory in the first leg in Budapest was a great team effort but Dennis' goal when he ran from the halfway line to score a wonderful solo effort really was something special.

Dennis was on target again in the home leg when he netted the only goal of the game to set up a tie against the crack Portuguese side Sporting Lisbon. The first leg was at Roker and we looked to be in control of the tie when we led 2-0 with only a few minutes remaining but a late strike brought Sporting back into the tie. To be honest the game should have been out of sight by then but it was one of those nights when we battered the opposition goal but simply couldn't add to our two-goal lead. Unfortunately, we'd missed our chance and our European adventure came to an end with a 2-0 defeat in Lisbon a couple of weeks later.

With our predicted promotion challenge failing to materialise I suppose it came as no surprise when the cup-winning team began to break up. We'd already lost Ritchie Pitt when he sustained an injury early in the season against Luton Town which effectively ended his career and in early March, Manchester City made their move and signed Dennis Tueart and Mickey Horswill, a deal which saw City midfielder Tony Towers joining us at Roker.

After the euphoria of the FA Cup win, the season had developed into one of huge disappointment although in fairness, just about every team we came up against seemed to raise their game against us. The mood in the dressing room wasn't particularly brilliant as the season drew to a close but I remember one hilarious incident in our final match of the season at Luton that had us all in stitches.

The comedian Eric Morecambe was their chairman at the time and just after we'd trooped into the dressing room at half-time the door opened and in he walked. "Bloody hell lads, if you can't beat that lot over there then you're not trying," he said, nodding towards the home dressing room across the corridor, "They're a set of prima donnas, they think they're world-beaters but they're not, I can tell you. Look at the goalkeeper, there's talk about him playing for England but he couldn't catch a cold and that number ten, bloody useless, can't trap a medicine ball. Then there's the centre-forward, what a plank, couldn't score in a brothel and what about that little midget on the wing, they daren't play him if it snows in case they lose him!"

The dressing room was in uproar but then he put on his glasses and slowly looked around the room briefly staring at the players one by one before declaring: "Oops, sorry lads - wrong dressing room!" That was typical of Eric, one of the greatest comedians in the history of show business and if you were ever in his company it was pretty certain that something like that was going to happen!

BILLY HUGHES TAKES ON THE SPORTING LISBON DEFENCE
DURING OUR 2-1 VICTORY OVER THE PORTUGUESE CUP-HOLDERS

ENJOYING THE LOCAL BREW DURING AN END OF SEASON HOLIDAY IN MAJORCA IN MAY 1973

A few days after that game rumours began to circulate that Sunderland were about to sign Bobby Moncur from Newcastle United and perhaps more importantly from my perspective, it was suggested that he would be taking over the role of team captain. At first it was just the odd little snippet in the paper but as the days and weeks passed the story began to gather momentum. I'd asked Bob Stokoe if there was any truth in the stories but he was saying nothing and by then people were stopping me in the street to ask me if I was about to lose the captaincy. The thing had dragged on for weeks mainly because Moncur had joined ITV's World Cup panel, but it got to the point where I could take no more and I asked the boss for a showdown meeting.

Bob sat grim faced behind his desk while I explained exactly why I was so annoyed. "As I told you when you came to the club, the captaincy doesn't bother me," I began, "But if you're planning to sign another player to take over the role I would have thought someone at the club would have had the decency to put me in the picture. After all, I'm a senior player here now and it's becoming bloody embarrassing when people are continually stopping me to ask if the stories in the press are true"

Amazingly, Bob still refused to shed any light on the matter and all he would say was: "I can't tell you anything Bobby; you'll just have to wait and see." I couldn't believe his attitude towards me. After all, little more than a year earlier he'd been singing my praises and referring to me as his 'Little General.' Now I felt as though I was being cast aside to make way for his new signing.

When I arrived home that afternoon I was still seething and decided there and then to put in a transfer request. Even though I'd never previously had the slightest desire to leave Sunderland there was a matter of principle at stake and the following morning I handed in a brief letter requesting the club place me on the transfer list. It was one of the hardest decisions I've ever had to make and in the weeks that followed the thought of leaving Roker Park began to haunt me. Maybe a move would have doubled my wages but I'd never been particularly ambitious in that respect and had always been quite content picking up what I considered to be fairly decent money playing for the club I loved.

Just as the 1974 World Cup competition was drawing to a close, the signing of Bobby Moncur was duly completed and to rub salt in the wounds it was announced during one of his appearances on ITV's panel of experts! In all fairness, I had no axe to grind with Bobby who had an excellent reputation in the game and when he arrived at Roker Park we got on really well together. It was the club I was having a go at and fortunately matters finally came to a head when we headed up to Berwick for a pre-season friendly and I was able to discuss the situation with chairman Keith Collings.

BOBBY MONCUR

BILLY ELLIOTT - THE PLAYER

BILLY ELLIOTT - THE MANAGER

Keith accepted that the club could have handled the situation better but assured me that no one in the Roker Park boardroom wanted me to leave and I was still very much part of Bob Stokoe's plans. Basically that was all I wanted to hear and if Bob had handled the situation better the whole unsavoury business could have been avoided. We shook hands after I'd agreed to withdraw my transfer request and I have to confess to being more than a little relieved that I could now concentrate on the only thing that really mattered to me - playing for Sunderland!

Mind you, I wasn't the only one at loggerheads with the club around this time with Billy Elliott threatening to take the club to an industrial tribunal after he was sacked with the club giving no explanation for what was to truly unbelievable decision. There isn't a single member of the '73 squad or indeed any other player I know of from that era who doesn't owe a debt of gratitude to Billy Elliott. He was Sunderland through and through having played for the club during its famous 'Bank of England' days in the 1950s and as a coach he was absolutely superb, most days staying behind after training to help individual players with their game.

His relationship with Bob Stokoe had always seemed a little uneasy and he later told me that he felt it probably dated back to a Wear -Tyne derby match at Roker Park back in the 1950s when he'd bloodied Bob's nose during a bust-up in the tunnel at the end of game. Whether that was behind the club's decision to sack Billy I'm not sure, but he soon demonstrated his coaching credentials when he enjoyed a highly successful spell with Norwegian side Brann of Bergen.

Another change to the backroom staff came when Arthur Cox took up his first managerial post at Chesterfield although when Bob Stokoe appointed his replacement he could hardly have picked a more different character. Arthur's quiet, calculated approach to the game could hardly have been more opposed to that of his successor Ian McFarlane who had worked with the boss during his Carlisle days. Ian was a larger than life character and when he was in the room you certainly knew it - to say he was loud was certainly no understatement!

He was always full of fun and speaking personally, I thought he was terrific guy who created a great atmosphere in the dressing room apart from the fact that he was also a vastly experienced coach. However, I suspect his antics and somewhat colourful language can't have gone down too well with the directors whenever they were in his company and it soon became common knowledge that he was less than popular with the hierarchy in the Roker Park boardroom.

OPENING THE SCORING AGAINST MILLWALL DURING OUR 4-1 VICTORY AT THE DEN ON THE OPENING DAY OF THE 1974-75 SEASON

When the 1974-75 campaign kicked off, hopes of a serious promotion challenge were high, particularly after Bob Stokoe secured the signing of Bryan 'Pop' Robson from West Ham. Pop was a proven goal scorer who had begun his career with Newcastle United although he could hardly be described as a 'Magpie' having been born in Westbourne Terrace, literally a stone's throw from Roker Park!

BILLY HUGHES FIRES HOME HIS SECOND GOAL IN THE FIVE-GOAL THRILLER AGAINST MANCHESTER UNITED AT OLD TRAFFORD

The arrival of Pop gave our attack some much needed firepower and he ended up with 19 goals in a season that saw us come within a whisker of clinching promotion. Throughout the season our main rivals had been Aston Villa and Manchester United who had amazingly dropped out of the top flight. We had two tremendous games against Tommy Docherty's young side and the first encounter, a five-goal thriller at Old Trafford, was voted Match of the Day's 'Game of the Season'.

It was a game we really should have won and I'll always remember a wonderful goal from Billy Hughes when he played a 'one-two' with Pop before firing home an unstoppable shot in front of the Stretford End. That goal gave us a 2-1 half-time lead but United surged back after the break with two goals although there was more than a hint of offside with their third and decisive goal.

For the remainder of the game we hammered away at their goal and just couldn't conjure up the vital breakthrough. For the neutral it must have been great entertainment but that was of little consolation as we headed back to Wearside empty handed.

The following week we hammered Portsmouth 4-0 at Roker but what I remember most from that game was a wonderful solo goal from Dick Malone when he dribbled through the Pompey defence before rounding the 'keeper to slot the ball into the empty net. I doubt if there was a more popular player with the fans than Dick and he almost lifted the roof off when he scored! There were great celebrations in our dressing room after the game with Dick, not surprisingly, the centre of attention.

However, our joy was short-lived that night when news came through that Ian Porterfield had been involved in a serious car crash on his way home from the game and was now critically ill in hospital after suffering a fractured skull.

Fortunately Ian went on to make a full recovery although in the days that followed the accident there was an uneasy atmosphere in the dressing room until we heard he was out of danger. Ian was out of action for almost a year and we certainly missed his creativity in midfield which was perhaps one of the main reasons we failed to clinch promotion, finishing in fourth place, just two points behind Norwich City.

Dave Watson was now our star player and had become established as an England regular so it was no surprise when he severed his ties with the club and joined Manchester City during the 1975 close season. I know Dave had resisted previous suggestions of a move into the top flight in the hope that he would make it there with Sunderland but when our season again finished in disappointment no one could blame him for joining City.

IAN PORTERFIELD - A GREAT PLAYER AND AN EVEN GREATER FRIEND

MEL HOLDEN AND JEFF CLARKE

To be fair, Dave deserved to be playing at the top level because in all my years in the game I don't think I ever came across a more dedicated professional. Every day, he would stay behind after training working in the gym and out on the pitch to try and maintain optimum fitness and improve his game. At his peak there wasn't a better central defender in the English game.

Finding a replacement looked to be an impossible task for Bob Stokoe but as part of the deal that took Dave to Maine Road, a young centre half named Jeff Clarke joined us at Roker. No one knew much about Jeff when he arrived but he soon proved to be an astute acquisition by the boss and immediately slotted in alongside Bobby Moncur in the heart of our defence.

In the season that followed, Bobby's experience proved invaluable as he helped Jeff develop into a key member of our squad and a player who would go on to give the club great service in the years ahead.

Another player to arrive during the 1975 close season was Mel Holden, a tall Scottish centre forward who was signed from Third Division Preston North End. Mel had played against us the previous season when the Lancashire side knocked us out of the League Cup at Deepdale and had proved something of a handful scoring one of their goals in a 2-0 victory and generally giving Dave Watson a torrid time throughout the game.

As soon as he arrived we could see his natural ability even though he was occasionally prone to the odd clumsy lapse when he would mis-control the ball. Whilst we never thought much about it at the time, these lapses proved to be the early stages of motor neurone disease, a debilitating illness which would eventually take his life at the age of only twenty-six.

When he joined us at Roker, Mel was only twenty-one but he soon proved his worth as an accomplished number nine forging an excellent strike partnership with Pop Robson and during the 1975-76 season the pair shared twenty-five goals as we romped to the Second Division championship. It was third time lucky for Bob Stokoe who had come under increasing pressure to get the club back into the top flight and during the campaign his health began to suffer as a result.

In particular, he used to get blinding migraine attacks which would completely wipe him out and we'd often come into the dressing room to find him stretched out on the treatment table. These attacks became so bad that towards the end of the season Bob began to miss some our games leaving Ian McFarlane to take over the reins, which I know must have hurt him deeply because he was desperate to lead the team to promotion.

MALCOLM ALLISON IN TYPICAL GUISE, SHEEPSKIN, FEDORA AND NO DOUBT HOLDING A HUGE CIGAR

In a way the 1973 cup win had become something of a millstone around his neck and had raised expectation levels at the club and among our supporters to such an extent that I'm sure many people thought we just had to turn up to win matches. Ironically, the 1975-76 season saw Wembley and the FA Cup beckoning again after we'd knocked out First Division Stoke City in a dramatic extra-time victory in the fifth round with Mel and Pop netting the vital goals. It was another of Roker's great nights and when the draw for the quarter finals handed us a home tie with Third Division Crystal Palace it seemed as though the twin towers were in sight again.

Palace were managed by former Manchester City boss Malcolm Allison, a flamboyant character in every sense who absolutely loved publicity and I remember him walking out onto the pitch just after we'd finished our pre-match warm-up. Instead of going to the Palace fans up in the main stand, he slowly walked towards the Fulwell End to bait our supporters.

Standing there in the goalmouth wearing his famous fedora and smoking a huge cigar, he was clearly enjoying every bit of the abuse that was raining down on him and at one point a match pie thrown from the crowd narrowly missed him and landed on the goal-line next to the post. Undeterred, he wandered over, turned and back-heeled the pie over the line before raising a fist of celebration to the crowd - it was pure theatre!

The game itself soon turned into a one-sided affair as we more or less camped in the Palace half with the visitors posing virtually no threat to our goal but as chance after chance was missed, I began to wonder if it was going to be one of those days. At half-time Bob Stokoe was furious, but to be honest it was only our finishing that had let us down in a game we had totally dominated.

The second-half continued in the same vein but then Palace conjured up a breakaway down the right and when Peter Taylor crossed, Alan Whittle swiveled to volley home from close range. After that we pushed forward relentlessly looking for the equaliser but it wasn't to be our day and at the final whistle came the harsh realisation that we'd missed a golden opportunity of another visit to Wembley. As if to rub salt in our wounds, the semi-final draw paired Palace with Southampton, a team we would surely have fancied our chances against, a view that was reinforced a few weeks later when we hammered them 4-0 in the league at Roker Park.

Overall though, the 1975-76 season had been a terrific campaign during which we'd been almost invincible in the league at Roker, but the real highlight for me personally came a few days after our final home game against Portsmouth when I led the team out for my testimonial game against Leeds United.

To me, our rivals from Yorkshire had seemed the obvious choice as opposition, particularly with the 1973 FA Cup win still fresh in the memory, and when I approached them they agreed without hesitation although, in typical fashion they did me no favours on the park and ran out comfortable 2-0 winners. The Leeds team was pretty much the side that we'd beaten at Wembley three years earlier and over the years we've always kept in touch, meeting at charity golf days and such like without even the slightest hint of the animosity that used to surface just about every time we met during our playing careers.

My testimonial game remains one of the highlights of my Sunderland career and I'll always be indebted to the 25,000 or so fans that turned up to support me that night. Like most players I had my ups and downs over the years, but overall they'd given me terrific support during my time at the club and I'll never forget that.

Apart from the disappointment of the Palace game, I'm sure our supporters were more than happy with our performances throughout the promotion season and with the Second Division championship trophy now sitting proudly in the Roker Park boardroom, thoughts were already turning to our assault on the top flight. When the club had previously been promoted in 1964, the team had struggled badly in the First Division with the Roker directors being heavily criticized for refusing to strengthen the team with top-class players. Amazingly, the Sunderland board seemed to have chosen a similar policy as the 1976 close season passed without a single major signing and before a ball was kicked we were being tipped as potential relegation candidates.

The pressure certainly seemed to be telling on Bob Stokoe who appeared to be much more short-tempered than usual and at times he seemed desperate to stamp his authority on individual players. This fact was illustrated perfectly when a notice appeared on the dressing room wall stating that for the forthcoming pre-season photo call, all players must be clean-shaven. If I remember rightly Billy Hughes and I were sporting a moustache at the time but the only other player affected was Roy Greenwood who wore a full beard. Roy had joined us from Hull City midway through the previous season and whenever we'd played against him previously he'd always sported a beard, in fact we used to refer to him as the bearded winger!

Roy was understandably furious and rightly argued that there was no mention of Bob's dislike of facial hair when he agreed to sign for Sunderland a few months earlier. When he asked for an explanation the only answer the boss could give him was: "Well, if you have a beard, it makes referees notice you more!" Unbelievable really but Bob stuck to his guns and Roy, who had flatly refused to shave off his beard, was banned from the pre-season photo call. Strangely enough, Hughesy and I were allowed to join in, moustaches and all, so perhaps it was only beards that the boss had suddenly taken a dislike to!

A BEARDED ROY GREENWOOD APPEARS ON OUR TEAM LINE-UP PHOTOGRAPH AFTER ALL.
THIS WAS TAKEN ONLY A FEW DAYS BEFORE BOB STOKOE RESIGNED AS SUNDERLAND MANAGER

BACK ROW L-R: JOE BOLTON, JIM MONTGOMERY, MICK HENDERSON AND GARY ROWELL. MIDDLE ROW L-R: DICK MALONE, BARRY SIDDALL, JACK ASHURST, JEFF CLARKE AND JIM HOLTON. FRONT ROW L-R: BOBBY KERR, BILLY HUGHES, TONY TOWERS, RAY TRAIN AND ROY GREENWOOD

LUNDI 10 MAI 1976

LA DEPÊCHE

DE TAHITI, LES ANG

LUNDI 10 MAI

LA

ON TOUR IN TAHITI DURING THE 1976 CLOSE SEASON

76

PAGE SPORTIVE

LAIS ONT JUSTIFIE L

A RARE MOMENT OF HARMONY WITH NEW BOSS JIMMY ADAMSON

We got off to a reasonable start to our first season back in the top flight with three draws in our opening games which suggested we might just be good enough to hold our own but only one point from the following seven games set the alarm bells ringing. By this stage Bob was under enormous pressure and had brought in Jim Holton and Alan Foggon from Manchester United to try and help turn our fortunes around but all to no avail.

Then amazingly the boss decided a change of goalkeeper was required and promptly signed Barry Siddall from Bolton Wanderers. If we had a weakness then it most certainly wasn't between the posts where Monty was still performing heroics and he would soon go on to prove he was still a more than capable 'keeper when he moved to Midlands club Birmingham City. To me, casting Monty aside was a clear sign that the boss was beginning to panic at our precarious position at the foot of the table.

Siddall made his debut in the 1-0 home defeat at home to Aston Villa which turned out to be the final nail in Bob's coffin and shortly afterwards it was announced that he was leaving the club by mutual consent. Whilst his departure came as no surprise, it was still upsetting for those of us who had been around since he first breezed into Roker Park in November 1972 to launch the club into arguably the greatest season in its entire history.

Football can be a cruel business and it was sad to see the man the fans had named 'The Messiah' not so very long before, now leaving the club in such a disappointing manner. Also, it was hard to imagine that Dick Malone, Billy Hughes and I were now the last remnants of the team that had taken English football by storm a little over three years earlier, a team that I'm certain would have gone on to achieve even greater things had they stayed together.

In the immediate aftermath Ian McFarlane was appointed caretaker manager and whilst we managed to record victories over Coventry City and Spurs, there was never any likelihood that he would be given the job on a permanent basis.

Instead the club turned to Burnley boss Jimmy Adamson to revive our fortunes, a man who had spent his entire career at Turf Moor and had actually played under Alan Brown when he was in charge of the Lancashire club back in the 1950s. Adamson's managerial credentials were certainly impressive and apparently at one point he was on the short list for the England job.

Almost from day one though, it became pretty obvious that our new boss had little time for the '73 lads and Hughesy was the first to leave when he was transferred to Derby County only a matter of weeks after Adamson's arrival.

BARRY SIDDALL

I'M MOBBED BY MY TEAMMATES AFTER NETTING A LATE EQUALISER AGAINST NORWICH CITY AT CARROW ROAD
A POINT WHICH GAVE OUR FIRST DIVISION SURVIVAL HOPES A MAJOR BOOST

Dick Malone only played a couple of games before being replaced by Mick Docherty who had arrived from Burnley and Adamson soon returned to his old club again to sign Colin Waldron and Doug Collins. Dick never played for Sunderland again and although I was still being selected, I was beginning to get the feeling that sooner or later I'd be the next to go. Adamson's arrival had brought no improvement in results and as well as failing to win any of his first ten games in charge, we hadn't even managed to score a goal.

Perhaps in desperation, he decided to turn to the younger players at the club and gave debuts to Shaun Elliott and Kevin Arnott. They joined Gary Rowell who had broken into the first team the season before. Their impact proved to be amazing as we set off on an incredible run that turned our season around almost overnight. Mel Holden had scored our first goal in nearly eleven games when he headed the winner against Bristol City but the real transformation came in three consecutive home games when we netted no fewer than sixteen goals. Those victories over Middlesbrough, West Brom and West Ham gave us a great chance of survival and our run of good form continued pretty much for the rest of the season with our final destiny hinging on the last game against Everton at Goodison Park.

The other two teams embroiled in the relegation battle were Coventry City and Bristol City who were meeting each other at Highfield Road on the same night. All we needed was a draw to survive but on the night we let our supporters down badly with Everton recording a comfortable 2-0 victory. Everything now hinged on the result of the other game which we discovered had inexplicably kicked off fifteen minutes late.

This meant Coventry and Bristol knew our final score before their game had ended and were able to play out a 2-2 draw, the only result that could put us down. There were tears in our dressing room when we heard the result from Highfield Road and many of our players, particularly the younger lads, felt we had been cheated.

Much has been written about the events of that evening and I have to confess it did leave something of a bad taste, but I've always maintained that we were in control of our own destiny and on the night we simply couldn't rise to the occasion.

Surprisingly I was pretty much a regular during the following season although Dick had predictably severed his ties with the club when he'd joined Bob Stokoe who'd returned to Blackpool to take over as manager. Sadly, I was now the last remaining member of the '73 squad although, in all honesty I was just happy to be getting regular first team football. The season went reasonably well and we finished the campaign in a respectable sixth place although we were never serious promotion challengers.

MICK DOCHERTY CAN'T BELIEVE IT - A 2-0 DEFEAT AT EVERTON IN THE FINAL GAME OF THE 1976-77 SEASON CONFIRMS OUR RELEGATION AFTER ONLY ONE SEASON BACK IN THE TOP FLIGHT

Although Jimmy Adamson and I had never really got on, I have to confess his coaching sessions were a breath of fresh air and often akin to those of Alan Brown with different routines being introduced almost every day. He was always a great one for tactical training in preparation for a forthcoming match when we would practise specific moves on the main training pitch at the Northumbria Centre although on one occasion his plans were thwarted in somewhat bizarre circumstances!

When we turned up for training on the morning in question we were greeted by a scene of absolute devastation with our training pitch completely churned up by what we assumed had been joy riders the night before. Adamson was going spare, ranting and raving about the 'youth of today' and such like and what he would do to them if he could get his hands on them. Eventually, when he'd calmed down, he led us into the gym and the session took place indoors with little more being said on the incident. It was only the following day that I learned that real culprits weren't joy riders at all, it had actually been our full back Joe Bolton and his dogs Jip and Tag!

Joe was pretty keen on hunting and such like and had decided that the open fields abutting our training complex were ideal territory for catching rabbits. Apparently he had an old van with a huge searchlight rigged up in the back which he would use to pick out the rabbits in the dark before setting the dogs off in hot pursuit. I'm not sure how long he'd been doing this but on this particular night he'd parked his van slap bang in the middle of our main training pitch and when he set off to leave he discovered the vehicle had sunk up to its axles in mud.

Apparently he'd spent ages attempting to drive the vehicle out but only succeeded in churning up the pitch even more. Finally he was forced to admit defeat and walk to the nearest phone box to summon help and eventually one of his mates turned up with a Land Rover to pull him out. I'm not sure whether Jimmy Adamson ever found out the truth about his wrecked training pitch, but the rest of the lads thought it was brilliant!

Whilst Jimmy Adamson may have been an excellent coach, his man -management skills certainly left a lot to be desired, as I would soon find out to my cost. As the 1978-79 campaign got underway it was pretty obvious that my days at the club were numbered and although I played in the first four games of that season, I suddenly found myself out in the cold. My final appearance in the famous red and white shirt came in a 2-0 defeat at Stoke City in the League Cup, and after that I spent the best part of six months waiting for the move that would get me playing first team football again.

JIMMY ADAMSON

Typically, Adamson was being less than helpful and whilst it was common knowledge that I was available for transfer, he insisted that there had been no inquiries. More importantly, he'd made it pretty obvious that he wasn't prepared to help arrange a move for me, unbelievable considering he clearly wanted me out of the club.

Then, out of the blue I received a phone call from my brother George asking if I would be interested in a move to Peterborough Utd. He said he knew their manager John Barnwell quite well and whilst it would mean a step down to Division Three, he assured me they were an excellent club. I told George I felt I was still capable of playing at a higher level but having become so disillusioned with the situation at Roker Park, I was prepared to consider anything. A week or so later George rang again, although this time he wasn't particularly happy. "Why the hell have you turned down Peterborough," he raged, "You told me you'd consider anything and now I've been made to look a right fool because you're refusing to even speak to them!" I was absolutely stunned and explained to George that I'd heard nothing since our last conversation but he insisted that whilst Peterborough hadn't made an official approach, the word from Jimmy Adamson was that I didn't want to talk to them and that was the end of the matter.

I was furious, and stormed in to see Adamson the next morning demanding an explanation although predictably, he denied all knowledge of the Peterborough approach. Sitting opposite him across the desk that morning, it occurred to me that perhaps his days at Sunderland were numbered as well. It was common knowledge within the club that the pressure in the Roker Park hot-seat had really began to affect him and the season before, supporters had started to question his commitment to the club when he refused to move from his home in Burnley.

Also, not for the first time, Brian Clough was being strongly linked with the Sunderland manager's job and group of supporters had even began a campaign to bring him and his assistant Peter Taylor to the club prompting Adamson to say famously: "I'm being hounded out of the job by a man who isn't even here!" Predictably, a few weeks later, he quit the club to take over the vacant manager's job at Leeds United and, speaking personally, I was glad to see the back of him!

After that I was pretty much in limbo until none other than Bob Stokoe came to my rescue and offered me the chance to team up with my old mate Dick Malone at Blackpool. To be honest I had no hesitation in making the move and whilst they were in the Third Division at the time I was offered a significant increase in salary as well as a brand new Ford Granada. It was a beautiful car and brilliant to drive but one morning when I was travelling over from Wearside I was involved in a crash just as I left the M6 at Garstang. Fortunately the car was still driveable but as you might imagine I received a great reception from my new colleagues when I pulled up outside Bloomfield Road in the battered Granada!

CLOUGH & TAYLOR: THE MEN THE FANS WANTED IN THE ROKER PARK HOT-SEAT

FIRING A SHOT IN ON GOAL FOR BLACKPOOL AT PLYMOUTH ARGYLE, SEPTEMBER 1979

DICK MALONE AND I PICTURED OUTSIDE THE BLACKPOOL FC CLUB SHOP SHORTLY AFTER TEAMING UP WITH OUR FORMER BOSS BOB STOKOE

Blackpool had arranged for me to move into the same digs as Dick Malone and not long afterwards another former Roker Park colleague, Jackie Ashurst, joined us there after signing for the club. Jackie was a quiet lad and never one for the night life although the same couldn't be said for Dick and I and most nights we'd wander along to the Tangerine Club adjacent to Bloomfield Road. The club was run by the supporters and whilst we tried to give the impression that we'd drink nothing other than non-alcoholic beverages, we always made sure there was a steady supply of wine cunningly concealed under the table!

Apart from those two broken legs early in my career, I'd pretty well managed to steer clear of serious injury but after only a matter of weeks at Bloomfield Road it looked as though my playing days might be over after a bizarre incident in a league game against Bury. I'd played a 'one-two' which had sent me through on goal and as I was about to feint to the left before checking back to shoot for goal, I inexplicably stood on the ball which flipped me into the air before sending me crashing to the ground. It must have looked hilarious and as I lay on the pitch unable to move I noticed most of the lads, including my good pal Dick Malone, were in fits of laughter.

Typically, as I was stretchered off the pitch I was getting little sympathy and even our physio seemed to see the funny side of the incident. However, I soon found myself in an ambulance heading off to hospital and it was only when I woke up the following morning that the real pain began to kick in.

My legs were fine but the rest of my body, particularly around my waist was wracked in pain and it was only after a series of x-rays that the doctors were able to establish the full details of the injury, a dislocated hip joint for which the only remedy was ten weeks in traction. I remember picking up the local newspaper the following day and reading that the specialist had referred to my injury as being 'of road traffic accident proportions'!

I was moved to Wrightington Hospital in Wigan which specialised in hip injuries and whilst their doctors and nursing staff were absolutely brilliant with me, those twenty weeks turned out to be the worst of my life; in fact I still have nightmares about bedpans and enemas! It got to the point where I was pleading with the nurses to let me get up but they assured me the treatment was essential if I wanted to make a full recovery and continue playing. Eventually, the day arrived when I was allowed to sit in the chair but the real relief came when I managed to get my bowel movements back to normal! To be honest I'd become pretty depressed until one day when I was sitting out on the veranda and spotted two strapping lads wandering over carrying a couple of slabs of Norsman lager.

ATTACKING THE GILLINGHAM DEFENCE, NOVEMBER 1979

CELEBRATING WITH THE FANS AFTER SCORING IN THE ANGLO SCOTTISH CUP AGAINST BURNLEY

It turned out they were Vaux draymen who had been delivering in the Manchester area and when they heard of my predicament they'd decided to pop in to see me. After that they would turn up every Tuesday afternoon, come rain or shine, with my supply of liquid refreshment. Since they were both keen Sunderland fans we always had plenty to talk about and when I was able to walk again I even travelled back to Wearside with them a couple of times. Over the years I lost touch with the two lads but I'll always be indebted to them for those weekly visits when they helped lift my spirits no end and set me on the road to recovery.

When I was discharged from hospital, the prospect of playing again seemed a long way off particularly after I'd been advised that a return to the top level game could have serious long-term implications to the injury. For a while I tried to face up to the prospect of not playing again but as I gradually regained fitness under the watchful eye of the medical staff at Blackpool, the prospect of resurrecting my playing career became increasingly attractive.

However, it soon became obvious that I no longer figured in first team affairs at Bloomfield Road and when I received a phone call from Hartlepool boss Billy Horner asking me if I fancied a return to the North East, I was soon packing my bags and heading home. To be honest Hartlepool suited me perfectly and whilst it was a drop down to the Fourth Division, I relished the prospect of playing again regularly and during my two years at the club, I enjoyed my football enormously.

Being able to live back at home was a terrific bonus and the thirty -minute journey down the coast to Hartlepool was a great relief after enduring those weekly pilgrimages across the country to Blackpool. At the time the former Newcastle defender John Bird was at the club and we used to travel down together picking up Phil Brown in South Shields along the way. Phil was a more than decent defender but never made it beyond the lower leagues although in more recent times he did succeed in carving out an impressive reputation in football management.

In the summer of 1982 my contract at Hartlepool came to an end and I was forced to face up to the prospect of earning my living outside of football, a harsh prospect given that I'd known nothing else since travelling down to Sunderland as a fifteen year old in 1964. My football continued in the local leagues which didn't bother me in the least because I've always enjoyed playing the game whether it's at Wembley or the nearest piece of waste ground!

Other than that I was spending most of my spare time desperately searching for full-time employment when a chance conversation with my old Sunderland teammate Jimmy McNab opened up an opportunity selling insurance.

Jim had just started working for a Newcastle-based company who were keen to capitalize on his football reputation and when he told them I might be interested we were soon working as a team, the pair of us targeting friends and associates on Wearside. As footballers, people had always welcomed our company but when it came to trying to persuade them to part with money their reaction was totally different and we soon discovered the meaning of the term: 'Yesterday's Hero.' In fairness, we did manage to do some decent business and having subsequently spoken to those people who took out policies, it seems they were fairly happy with their returns. However, it soon became apparent that perhaps I wasn't particularly cut out for the insurance game and when the opportunity arose I chose the path followed by many ex-players by moving into the pub trade.

The approach came from Cameron's Brewery and the pub they offered me was Oscars in Hartlepool, a decent business as things turned out even if it did take me a while to learn how demanding the licensing trade can be. In those first few months I was working around the clock but enjoying every minute particularly the banter with the locals.

After about six months I'd managed a week away in the sun and returned with a wonderful bronzed tan prompting one of the punters to take my photograph which soon appeared on the wall in the bar with the caption 'Juan'. Each night when they were leaving they'd all be shouting: 'Goodnight Juan' and I have to confess that it was a few days before the penny dropped and I suddenly realised what they were actually calling me was 'Juan Kerr!'

After Oscars, the pub trade dominated my life with a procession of tenancies providing steady employment however, it was also during this time that my life entered a tumultuous period on the domestic front when my marriage to Cathy broke up, finally ending in divorce. I'd met a lady by the name of Linda Kirtley and immediately decided that I wanted to spend the rest of my life with her. We were married on 24th December 1987 and four years later our son James was born - I'd never been happier.

On the business front we'd taken over The Copt Hill public house in Houghton-le-Spring on the outskirts of Sunderland and with business booming, the brewery were soon extending the premises to incorporate a restaurant and function room. As far as the business side was concerned, Linda and our partner Mark Hird pretty much ran the show, while I was more than happy to rub shoulders with the punters on the other side of the bar. The Sunderland Former Players Association began holding their monthly meetings there and soon the place became a regular haunt for Sunderland stars both past and present which was brilliant for business of course!

SHARING A DRINK WITH MY OLD MATE HUGHESY

SUNDERLAND LEGENDS NIGHT AT THE SEABURN HOTEL, MAY 1993

OPENING THE COLONEL PRIOR PUBLIC HOUSE WITH 1937 LEGENDS, RAICH CARTER, BOBBY GURNEY AND LEN DUNS

AXA

Niall Quinn was regular visitor, a brilliant guy who basically just wanted to enjoy a good drink and be one of the lads. Outside of football Niall's passion was horse-racing and he was beginning to enjoy some success with his own horses which he trained at his stables near Sedgefield. One night he turned up at the Copt Hill with a jockey who was riding one of his mounts at Wetherby the following day and the two of them drank well into the night with Quinny consuming his usual quota of Guinness!

By the time he was ready to leave the big fella was in high spirits and decided to hoist the wee jockey onto his shoulders as he made his way out to the car park. What he hadn't reckoned on however, was the low height of the main door and the poor jockey ended up cracking his head against a glass display case above the door before toppling backwards onto the floor. He was out cold for some minutes before slowly regaining consciousness and it was hardly surprising that he was unable to race the following day with the official announcement stating that he was suffering from concussion following an accident at home the day before!

Of course, 1973 was always a regular topic with punters who visited the pub and in May 2000 memories of that great day came flooding back when Linda and I were invited to Wembley's last FA Cup final before the old stadium was pulled down. AXA were the competition sponsors at the time and they'd invited FA Cup-winning captains along to mark the occasion. Apart from myself, there was Tony Adams, Billy Bonds, Ron Harris, Frank McLintock and Martin Buchan and we all met up at the Wembley Conference Centre prior to the game where we were interviewed in turn by Brian Moore.

Basically, we each recalled our memories of our particular finals which were put out live to corporate guests on giant screens and I remember talking about how I forgot to pick up my medal and then fell down the steps almost dropping the trophy! Brian Moore was a lovely guy who I got to know pretty well during the '73 cup run and when he first spotted me all he could say was: 'Bobby Kerr ...Bobby Kerr!'

Around 2 o'clock we were heading down Olympic Way to the stadium when we encountered a guy wearing these huge ear-muffs who'd obviously been drinking heavily and as he staggered towards us he stopped and slowly pointed at Billy Bonds before saying: "Hey you ...I know you ...your name's Billy isn't it?" The guy was in such a state that he could hardly stand up let alone recognize anyone, yet as we tried to pass him he grabbed hold of Billy's jacket shouting: "You're that Billy Bonds aren't you? You are ...you're that Billy Bonds!" By now Billy was getting pretty fed up but still the guy wouldn't let us pass until finally the former West Ham skipper told him exactly where to go in typical Cockney fashion!

WEMBLEY STADIUM, MAY 2000
FORMER MANCHESTER UNITED SKIPPER MARTIN BUCHAN AND I POSE WITH THE FA CUP

1981 FA CUP FINAL, WEMBLEY, 9TH MAY 1981. TOTTENHAM HOTSPUR 1 MANCHESTER CITY 1
THIRTY FORMER FA CUP-WINNING CAPTAINS WERE INVITED TO MARK CELEBRATIONS FOR THE 100TH FA CUP FINAL
L-R: DAVE MACKAY (TOTTENHAM HOTSPUR, 1967), DANNY BLANCHFLOWER (TOTTENHAM HOTSPUR, 1961 AND 1962)
DICK PYM (BOLTON WANDERERS, 1923, 1926 AND 1929, NOT CAPTAIN BUT ONE OF THE OLDEST SURVIVING FINALISTS), PAT RICE (ARSENAL, 1979)
PETER RODRIGUES (SOUTHAMPTON, 1976), BOBBY KERR (SUNDERLAND 1973), GRAHAM WILLIAMS (WEST BROMWICH ALBION, 1968)
RON YEATS (LIVERPOOL, 1965), NOEL CANTWELL (MANCHESTER UNITED, 1963), JACK BURKITT (NOTTINGHAM FOREST 1959)
JOHNNY DIXON (ASTON VILLA, 1957), JIMMY SCOULAR (NEWCASTLE UNITED, 1955), JOE MERCER (ARSENAL 1950)
JOHNNY CAREY (MANCHESTER UNITED, 1948), TOM SMITH (PRESTON NORTH END, 1938) AND RONNIE STARLING (SHEFFIELD WEDNESDAY, 1935)

LINDA AND I - I'D NEVER BEEN HAPPIER

That incident aside, the day was brilliant and the AXA people looked after us wonderfully well even though it was quite a demanding schedule at times. As things turned out I spent most of the time with Martin Buchan and even though we'd never actually met previously we seemed to hit it off really well together. Linda and I had decided to stay in central London so we could meet up with my pal David Armstrong, the former Middlesbrough and Southampton player who'd travelled up from his home on the south coast. David and I had been close pals for years and we spent the night before the final at our hotel catching up on old times over a few drinks. It was only on the morning of the match that we discovered how difficult it was going to be to get from inner London and out to Wembley on cup final day and even though it was a relatively short distance the taxi journey took well over an hour!

As we entered the new millennium, life promised so much for Linda, James and I and at the time I remember thinking that things really couldn't have been much better. Then, on 31st October, I was at home at our house at Moorside when I received a phone call that would change my life forever.

Linda had headed off earlier in the day to do some shopping at The Galleries in Washington when suddenly the phone rang with a policeman asking if I knew if she was on any sort of medication. Other than that he would tell me nothing other than she'd been taken ill, however soon afterwards I spotted a police car pulling up outside the house and as I walked down the drive towards him I pretty much feared the worst. "You're going to tell me my wife's died aren't you?" I asked and when he replied: "Can we go inside please sir?", I knew I'd lost her.

It turned out she'd had a heart attack and died almost instantly and I now faced the job of breaking the news to James when I picked him up from school later that afternoon. He was only eight-years-old and I don't think I'll ever face a more difficult task as long as I live. How we got through the months after that I'll never know but we did, although I'll never forget the help and support we were given by our friends and family - without them I couldn't honestly say I'd have survived. My only concern after losing Linda was to see James come through the heartbreak unscathed and I'm proud to say that he's now developed into a fine young man.

Linda's death capped a terrible period for the Kerr family with my brothers George and Bill both losing their wives and soon afterwards I received the news that Bill had also passed away. To receive so much devastating news in such a short space of time, was probably the start of my downfall as far as The Copt Hill was concerned. Linda had pretty much ran the business side and I now had to rely on other people to run things for me although it's no criticism of their efforts because at the end of the day I fully accept that the pub's ultimate failure was solely my responsibility and I know now that I was spending far too much time on the wrong side of the bar.

THE OLD GUY CAN STILL DO IT! PLAYING FOOTY WITH JAMES IN THE BACK GARDEN OF OUR HOUSE AT MOORSIDE

JAMES AND I SHOW OFF THE KERR TARTAN

TEEING OFF AT ONE OF THE SUNDERLAND FORMER PLAYERS ASSOCIATION'S CHARITY GOLF DAYS

Nevertheless, I was still desperate for the place to succeed, so much so that I foolishly sold our house on Moorside and ploughed the money straight into the business in a forlorn attempt to keep things afloat. It worked for a while but in 2008 the money simply ran out and soon afterwards came the shattering news that I'd been declared bankrupt. The brewery immediately terminated the tenancy and as we'd been living over the pub, James and I were left with the stark prospect of having nowhere to live.

I'd now reached the lowest ebb of my entire life and yet again it was my friends who helped me survive and I'll always be eternally grateful to everyone who came to my rescue. I make no excuse for the predicament I found myself in, it was my own doing no question and I was very fortunate that people still had sufficient faith in me to rally round and support me through a truly horrendous time. My former colleagues to a man were brilliant, my good pal Dave Hegarty couldn't have been more supportive and I'll always be grateful to Mickey Scott and the Moran brothers, Eric, Colin, David and Steve for sorting out accommodation and setting up benefit payments and such like for me. I'm not proud that I now have to rely on the state to survive, just grateful that my life is stable again and that James is safely on the road to what I hope and pray will be a happy and successful life of his own.

As far as my football career is concerned, I had the good fortune to play with some of the finest players in the English game and when people ask me who was the greatest, I always tell them that in terms of pure ability no one compared with Jim Baxter, a true genius but sadly, a flawed character. Then there's Charlie Hurley, a giant of a man in every sense and of course my good mate Jim Montgomery, so many times have I seen him defy the opposition with his heroics, a truly brilliant 'keeper.

As far as opposition players go, I don't think I ever came up against a finer player than George Best, an unbelievable talent and a player who could and should have achieved so much more in the game. For me though, the greatest player I ever saw was Alfredo Di Stefano and I'll never forget the 1960 European Cup final at Hampden Park when he and Ferenc Puskas shared seven goals to destroy Eintracht Frankfurt in the greatest display of attacking football I ever saw.

These days, people often ask me if I have any regrets and I always say that as far as football is concerned I wouldn't change a thing. Of course, our achievements in 1973 will always be the highlight of my time in football and I'm delighted to say that the team spirit that was so important during the cup run still remains to this day. When we played together, the '73 squad were pals both on and off the pitch and even today we still meet up regularly through the Sunderland Former Players Association.

WITH THE LEGENDARY CHARLIE HURLEY JUST AFTER HE'D BEEN VOTED 'SUNDERLAND'S PLAYER OF THE CENTURY' AT THE MAYFAIR BALLROOM IN NOVEMBER 1979

MEMBERS OF THE 1973 FA CUP-WINNING SQUAD AT THE STADIUM OF LIGHT CELEBRATING THE 40TH ANNIVERSARY OF OUR VICTORY OVER LEEDS UNITED

Sadly two of the men who figured prominently that season are no longer with us. I was deeply saddened when Bob Stokoe died in 2004 and perhaps even more so when Ian Porterfield lost his battle with cancer three years later.

Ian and I had been good friends since he arrived at Roker Park back in 1968 and the last time I saw him was when I travelled down to London with Monty, Dick Malone and Mickey Horswill to visit him in hospital. Typically of Ian, he was in good spirits but to see him looking so poorly really was traumatic. If nothing else that sort of experience puts life in perspective and it certainly made me reflect that perhaps my life these days isn't really so bad after all.

Nowadays, I've pretty much settled for the quiet life although I am kept pretty busy doing charity work with the Sunderland Former Players Association as well as entertaining corporate guests at the Stadium of Light on match days. Even now, after all these years, there's hardly a day goes by when someone doesn't ask me about 1973 and to be fair I never tire of the subject. After all, I'm still the only man alive to have lifted a major trophy for Sunderland Football Club and to have been part of what was probably the club's greatest ever achievement is something I'll cherish until the day I die.

"Football has left me with numerous wonderful memories but none can compare with the moment of sheer joy when the final whistle blew at Wembley on 5th May 1973!"